Praise for
LEFT STANDING

Mason's journey of faith is truly inspiring.

—RICHARD PAUL EVANS, #1 *New York Times* best-selling
author of *The Christmas Box* and the Michael Vey series

Mason Wells's story is a powerful endorsement of the power of faith to shield us from unimaginable pain and horror while sparking encouragement from a reservoir of hope that resides deep within each of us. I want to study every page of this compelling book to see how I can learn from Mason . . . so I can make my own life better by nurturing a faith like his.

—SQUIRE RUSHNELL, *New York Times* best-selling author
of the GodWink series

Mason Wells's testimony is one that reminds us where "Why me God?" is simply answered "Why not you?"—where with true faith there can be blessings beyond the battles. Being caught in the crosshairs and the chaos of the enemy can bring supernatural healing and restoration. A memoir for the ages.

—JONATHAN CAIN, keyboardist for the band Journey

LEFT STANDING

The Miraculous Story of How Mason Wells's Faith Survived
the Boston, Paris, and Brussels Terror Attacks

LEFT STANDING

The Miraculous Story of How Mason Wells's Faith Survived
the Boston, Paris, and Brussels Terror Attacks

MASON WELLS
TYLER BEDDOES & BILLY HALLOWELL

PLAIN SIGHT
PUBLISHING

An Imprint of Cedar Fort, Inc.
Springville, Utah

ISBN 13: 978-1-4621-2158-8

Published by Plain Sight Publishing, an imprint of Cedar Fort, Inc.
2373 W. 700 S., Springville, UT 84663
Distributed by Cedar Fort, Inc., www.cedarfort.com

LIBRARY OF CONGRESS CATALOGING-IN-PUBLICATION DATA

Names: Wells, Mason, author. | Beddoes, Tyler, author. | Hallowell, Billy, author.
Title: Left standing : the miraculous story of how Mason Wells's faith survived the Boston, Paris, and Brussels terror attacks / Mason Wells, Tyler Beddoes, and Billy Hallowell.
Description: Springville, Utah : Plain Sight Publishing, an Imprint of Cedar Fort, Inc., [2017] | Includes bibliographical references.
Identifiers: LCCN 2017039171 (print) | LCCN 2017042524 (ebook) | ISBN 9781462128662 (ebook) | ISBN 9781462121694 (pbk.) | ISBN 9781462121588 (hardback dustjacket)
Subjects: LCSH: Wells, Mason. | Mormon missionaries--Biography. | Victims of terrorism--Biography. | Boston Marathon Bombing, Boston, Mass., 2013. | Terrorism--France--Paris--History--21st century. | Terrorism--Belgium--Brussels--History--21st century. | LCGFT: Autobiographies.
Classification: LCC BX8695.W454 (ebook) | LCC BX8695.W454 A3 2017 (print) | DDC 289.3092 [B] --dc23
LC record available at https://lccn.loc.gov/2017039171

Cover design by Jeff Harvey
Cover design © 2017 by Cedar Fort, Inc.
Edited by Kathryn Watkins and Kaitlin Barwick
Typeset by Kaitlin Barwick

Printed in the United States of America

10 9 8 7 6 5 4 3 2 1

Printed on acid-free paper

This book is dedicated to Isabel, Mari-Anne, Michael, and Veerle, for helping me in the toughest of times—and to all those affected by the Boston, Paris, and Brussels terror attacks.

—Mason Wells

Also by
TYLER BEDDOES

Proof of Angels (with Ptolemy Tompkins)

Also by
BILLY HALLOWELL

The Armageddon Code
Fault Line

CONTENTS

CONTENTS

ACKNOWLEDGMENTS

Mason Wells

First and foremost, I want to thank God for His merciful hand and unrestricted love.

To my parents, Chad and Kymberly, who were solid anchors during a storm no parent should have to brave.

To my siblings, Colby, Porter, Mia, and Tayla, the best brothers and sisters anyone could ask for.

To my incredible grandparents, aunts, uncles, and cousins, who were a source of strength throughout my recovery and continue to support my future endeavors.

To my grandfather and great-grandfather, who taught me through example what it means to be a man of integrity.

To my patient mission companions: Tyler Barber, Korban Lehman, Benjamin Quist, Daelin Johnson, Streiker Hoffmann, Matthew Jouffray, Jonah Griffith, and Joe "Dresden" Empey.

To Richard Norby, for remaining a stalwart example of overcoming adversity during hard times.

To my mission president, Frederic Babin, and his optimism that "tomorrow is the first day of the rest of your life," and his sincere belief that we can be vehicles for change.

To Tyler Beddoes, for inspiring me to believe that my story could, in fact, help other people.

To Billy Hallowell, for taking a chance on a naïve nineteen-year-old.

To Mike and Katy at Cedar Fort, for all of their effort and goodwill in sharing my story.

To my good friend, Colton Kasteler, for putting up with all of my bomb jokes (after it wasn't "too soon").

To Jeanette Bennett, as well as countless friends and neighbors, who took pressure off of my family in the days following the Brussels attack.

To anyone who ever prayed on behalf of me or my companions—we are eternally grateful.

Finally, my sincere gratitude to any person that has ever put their life in danger by attending to survivors of a terrorist attack. You have truly made the world a better place.

Tyler Beddoes

I would first like to thank God and my Lord and Savior Jesus Christ for giving me an amazing life. A big thank you to my wife, Brittany, and our three children, Gracie, Gunnar, and Ella, for being ever so patient and supportive and letting me take a lot of time away while working on this project. Brittany—you are my rock, and I love you so very much, and I want you to know that I couldn't have done this without you. I want to thank my parents, Dan and Pam, and

Grandma Anna for always being there for me and for being the great examples you all are; I love you dearly. To Grandpa Donald, Uncle Eddie, and all those guiding me from the heavens above—thank you and I love you!

A sincere thanks to my brother Zack and my sister-in-law Heidi for their kindness, support, and helping hands whenever I ask. You both are shining examples, and I look up to you both greatly. You mean the world to me. Zack—I want you to know that you are my hero in all walks of life, and I hope one day I can be more like you. To all my brothers- and sisters-in-law, and to all my family thank you and I love you. Thank you to my mother- and father-in-law, Shelly and Kirt, for your unwavering support, friendship, and love. I love you both!

I want to thank Mason for giving me the great opportunity to work on this project. It was a true pleasure working with you. You are so inspiring, and I have learned a great deal about the importance of faith, hope, and love while working with you. You made me a better and more loving person, and for that I am forever grateful. I look up to you greatly—love you my friend!

A big thanks to Chad and Kymberly Wells for your advice, support, phone calls, and encouragement. Chad—thanks for always putting a smile on my face whenever we communicated on the phone or in person. You and Kym are amazing people.

Thanks to Billy for your friendship and for being a great cowriter on this book. You are so very talented and are an amazing person and writer. Thanks for making me a better person and writer and for offering words of encouragement. I love and appreciate you.

A *big* thank you to everyone at Cedar Fort Publishing for believing in this project and having our backs. You have all been a joy to work with, and I am very thankful for you all in giving this book a great home.

Katy—you are an amazing editor and an even better person, and I appreciate you putting up with my endless calls and ideas throughout this process.

To all those affected by the Boston, Paris, and Brussels terrorist attacks, I will continually pray for you and your families, and know that you all sit heavy on my heart and mind. Remember to never give up and remain positive even in the toughest of times. To anyone that reads this book, thank you for your great support, and Godspeed to you all!

Billy Hallowell

I would like to acknowledge and profoundly and formally thank the following individuals and institutions, as this book would not have been possible without them:

First, thank you, Lord, for continuing to amaze me by paving for me such a fascinating and rewarding path—one that continues to surprise me.

Second, thank you to my wife, Andrea, and my kids, Ava and Lilyana, for allowing me the time to work on this project. Andrea, you are the most patient, loving, and amazing wife a guy could ask for. Thanks for your ceaseless support.

Mason, thank you for trusting me with your story—one that I believe will deeply impact many lives. And Tyler, I appreciate your friendship and your decision to bring me into this project. It continues to be an honor to get to know you both professionally and personally.

And thank you to Cedar Fort for allowing us to explore such a fundamentally important story. Your partnership in this endeavor has been wonderful.

Last—but most certainly not least—thank you to my parents, who have always believed in me and who fervently instilled in me the importance of embracing truth, sticking to my convictions, and standing for what's right.

Thank you all for making this book a reality.

FOREWORD
by Roma Downey

Emmy-nominated actress
from CBS's *Touched by an Angel*

There are certain stories that we encounter in life that have the power to pull at our heartstrings as they carry us along on a journey through the trials of tragedy to the joys of triumph.

Mason Wells's ordeal is one of those stories.

It's impossible not to feel deeply uplifted and profoundly touched by this young man's incredible and awe-inspiring story. His journey is one full of heart and devotion and shows us an unrivaled perseverance that is truly unique.

In *Left Standing: The Miraculous Story of How Mason Wells's Faith Survived the Paris, Boston, and Brussels Terror Attacks*, Wells shares the sights, sounds, and fears that he experienced firsthand at the site of the Boston Marathon bombing in 2013.

While that experience profoundly shaped Wells's young mind, in an extraordinary twist of fate, he went on to have two additional encounters with terror. He was serving as a missionary in Calais, France—only hours away from Paris—in November 2015 when terrorists killed 130 people and wounded hundreds of others.

Then, just months later, he was seriously injured while standing in line at the Brussels Airport—an experience that left him with dire injuries to his hand and foot as well as burns and shrapnel across his body.

The mental and physical anguish associated with the attack was difficult to contend with, as Mason went from a young nineteen-year-old with a plethora of life goals and opportunities to someone who found himself facing multiple layers of uncertainty, pain, and anxiety.

Everything from his future military service goals to his ability to simply jog and work out was suddenly in question, leaving him in an emotionally trying scenario.

But as readers will see in *Left Standing*, Mason has a determination to overcome the odds. From his persistence in recovery to his reflective thoughts that carry valuable insights and perspective far beyond his years, Mason teaches us all some important lessons about the power of the human spirit and the importance of embracing forgiveness.

Rather than harboring hate and resentment for the terrorists he tragically crossed paths with, Mason has chosen to respond with love and dignity, clinging to the hope that has so profoundly colored and shaped his young life.

Left Standing is his impassioned quest to share not only the details of what he faced, but also the lessons he's learned along the way.

You'll feel humbled at the end of the book as Mason and his decision to offer such deep forgiveness reminds us that we're all children of God capable of receiving the Father's love.

With so much pain in our world and so many people experiencing heartache and loss, Mason's story is inspiring because it proves that giving up simply isn't an option and that by forging on and pushing yourself to overcome, immeasurable growth and healing can follow.

I believe that Mason's story of hope, love, and overcoming incredible difficulty will touch your life in profound ways. In a sometimes dark and scary world, this true story of overcoming hate shines a bright light of hope. I'm incredibly grateful that Mason has chosen to share it with us.

—Roma Downey

PREFACE |
Survival |

*But the Lord stood at my side
and gave me strength.*
(2 Timothy 4:17, NIV)

All throughout my life, I've seen miracles. Miracles are by definition unexplainable, real-world manifestations of God's transcendent power. Some occur as a result of fervent prayer, and there are some that can only be chalked up to pure divine intervention. For the believer, miracles demonstrate the willingness of a loving God to protect and sustain His children. To others, they represent nothing more than happenstance in an otherwise disorganized world. I belong to the former school of thought.

The miraculous experiences of my young life, both large and small, have forged, sustained, and manifested in me a faith that I cannot deny. One such defining moment took place as I stood thunderstruck in a rapidly amassing pool of my own blood after scrambling from the Brussels Airport on March 22, 2016.

It was pure adrenaline that had carried me to safety outside the airport, where I suddenly stood frozen, flummoxed and terrified by the scene that lay before me. I was disoriented by the cacophony of injured and panicked men, women, and children. I was so overwhelmed by the chaos around me and the feedback I was getting from my own injured body that I stood motionless—detached and unable to comprehend what was occurring right in front of me.

Terrorists had just detonated two homemade bombs hidden inside suitcases in the Brussels Airport, killing more than thirty innocent people while injuring scores of others. I was among those injured in the attacks. It was a brush with death that would forever change my perspective, leaving physical and emotional scars to serve as constant reminders of the best and worst of mankind.

It is impossible to fully describe the emotions I felt shortly after the attacks. My basic survival instincts temporarily crowded out any other emotion. Despite sustaining second- and third-degree burns to my face and hand, shrapnel throughout my body, a broken left heel, and a ruptured Achilles tendon, I somehow survived.

And the story of my experience quickly captured the attention of the nation and the world. Once the US media discovered that I was an American citizen, I received dozens of requests for interviews. My story became even more captivating to the media once they learned that this was not my first brush with terror.

On April 15, 2013, three years before the Brussels incident, my family and I witnessed the horrors of the Boston Marathon bombing. While my dad and I cheered for my mom as she competed in the race, terrorists detonated two bombs near the finish line, taking the lives of 3 and wounding 260 others. Luckily, we were not injured in the blasts—not physically injured anyway. That act of senseless violence and hatred left a mark on my developing faith that took some time to heal.

Only two years after Boston, my second encounter with terror occurred in France. I had been extended the invitation from my church to provide Christian service to the people of France and surrounding areas for a period of two years. This experience was a new beginning for me, an opportunity to serve others while trying to forget the unwelcome events of Boston. My faith in God and in people was recovering when another blow shocked its tender roots.

Before the November 13, 2015, assault on Paris that killed 130 and wounded hundreds of others, I regularly made the trek to Paris and had observed firsthand some of the unrest that had been escalating at the time. I had no inclination that such a horrific terror attack would unfold and was stunned when it did. The fateful day arrived as terrorists wreaked havoc on the beautiful city of Paris. And though I was miles away in Calais when that happened, it was yet another act of violence that hit far too close to home and once again rekindled the fearful emotions I had tried to forget.

Only months later, my missionary assignment took me to Brussels where my third and most life-threatening grapple with extremism took place. Instead of witnessing the explosions from a distance of yards or miles, I was mere feet away from the epicenter. About ten feet away, as a matter of fact.

Within the pages of this book, I will explain the details and circumstances of each attack as I remember them.

The retelling of my experiences only led to more questions, for example: How could one young man have witnessed so many high-profile terror attacks and live to tell the tale? During my painful recovery, I entertained calls from several local and national news outlets such as Fox News, ABC News, 20/20, CNN, *Good Morning America*, CBS News, and many others. To date, I've remained relatively quiet, but now feel it is the right time to break my silence.

With the telling of my story, I deeply hope that the uninvited yet faith-solidifying life lessons I've learned through my experiences will serve to inspire many people to rise above despondency and despair and be filled with hope and optimism. This book is not about terror. It is not a book written to sensationalize or simply entertain. Nor can I give voice to the hundreds and thousands of others across the earth who have been victimized by the cruel acts of others. Rather, this book is about my journey of faith, hope, and love: a faith in God and the general goodness of humankind; a hope of better days to come; and a desire to extinguish the fear of hate with the power of love.

Through my experiences, I've learned deeper lessons than I ever imagined about the power of faith, perseverance, and unity. It is my goal to take you through the horrors I faced, while explaining the aftereffects of terror as well as the hope and healing that I found in the wake of the Brussels attack.

Since returning to Utah in April of 2016, including the thirty-seven days I spent in the hospital, I began formulating my own questions about life and about God. Externally, I was coping with serious, potentially crippling injuries. But internally, the emotional and spiritual effects ran deeper.

In the days and weeks following the Brussels attack, the gravity of the situation and the shock that I had somehow survived prompted a flood of questions: Why did I survive while many others inside the airport did not? Why did God allow me to live? Weren't there so many more better-suited people that the Lord could have chosen—people more prepared and more equipped to inspire and help others by later sharing their personal story of survival?

And one question surfaced at the center: What does God want for my future? This is a question most of us have probably asked at one point or another. To be honest, I have thought and prayed about my purpose on earth since I was a child. Yet the defining moment at Brussels launched a newfound curiosity that has set me on a quest to discover my contribution to humanity and what I am supposed to accomplish on earth. These questions never really leave me. Perhaps the insistent reminder of my injuries and the occasionally resurfacing emotional scars pull me up sharply to rethink my previous goals and aspirations. One of my goals was to one day join the US military: a goal that I have recently achieved.

We all face struggles of some degree. Many of us question what God wants for our lives and if there is a bigger purpose for us. So often life's obstacles feel monumental; our lives feel out of control. Our trials hold the power to overtake us and rock us to our core. Yet our trials can serve to refine us in ways that may otherwise be impossible. Perhaps more importantly, our pain can spur us on to help others who also suffer. I want to actively allow my ordeal to turn me outward with love rather than inward with sorrow. As I have imperfectly strived to make this conscious choice—to dwell upon faith, forgiveness, and hope—I have found a larger purpose for my life and a desire to lift others out of despair. Perhaps if it is possible for me to forgive those responsible for altering my life, it is also possible for me to help others forgive those who have wronged them.

I'm convinced that in some way or another, every one of us can be a saving grace in the life of someone else. The challenges I've faced happened in a dramatic way but the challenges themselves are not unique. We all experience pain, disappointment, frustration, and anger to one degree or another. The decision to confront these feelings—the decision to have courage—can turn the bad things in our favor if we can let go of our pain and heartache and let God guide our happiness.

I'm also a firm believer that light always triumphs over darkness—even when evil fervently attempts to stomp out the flame of goodness. In the end, despite my struggles and the nightmare I endured, I am adamant about my belief that hope, on this side of heaven, is the primary antidote to fear. As our faith exceeds our fears, we will be more inclined to make the changes in our own lives that will lead to a better world, a more God-filled world.

CHAPTER 1
Preparation

*Before anything else, preparation
is the key to success.*
—Alexander Graham Bell[1]

I can attribute my survival and continued faith to two factors: God and my family. And that is a chicken-and-egg situation, as my parents built their home with the Savior as its foundation. So from an early age, my parents instilled in me the values of faith, family, and virtue. I am eternally grateful to my parents for providing me with this sure foundation, as it has steadied me during the moments where my faith and resolve were shaken.

Looking back on the unfinished tapestry of my life, I can clearly see the vibrant threads—occurrences and personal experiences—that wove together to catch and prepare me for Boston, Brussels—and beyond. It is as I examine the colorful portions of the cloth that represents my childhood and the progression of my early life that I'm able to see how God was at the loom—looping and threading the strands of me together, preparing my heart and mind for what was to come.

Growing up in the suburbs, I had your typical white-picket-fence experience. I am the oldest of five kids, ranging in age from twenty to four. I grew up in a two-story home in a neighborhood that offered up plenty of places for me to explore.

As a child, I was relatively reserved, and at my core, I was a rule-follower. My parents set the parameters—and I, in large part, followed them. I was probably more empathetic as a kid, having perhaps even more sensibilities at the

The Wells family.

time than I do now. I didn't like seeing people unhappy, and I still don't.

While empathy was a key element of my personality, I also liked discipline, a rare quality for a kid. It wasn't entirely surprising, though, when you really think about it. My family has always embraced a culture of discipline and love. My parents were and are the two greatest exemplars of these two attributes.

I always knew that my father loved me unconditionally. When I was younger, he put hours and hours into coaching my sports teams. When he was home, he was focused on my siblings and me, teaching by example what love and devotion truly look like. Meanwhile, my mom, who came from a military family, carried with her the structured values she learned while growing up. She enforced a chore schedule, cooked our meals, and saw us off to school every single day, among a million other selfless acts I probably overlooked entirely at the time.

Considering the intricate balance of love, devotion, tradition, discipline, and structure, perhaps it's no surprise that, at a very young age, I became consumed with the military, and more specifically, the US Marines. My grandfather, a retired colonel, and my great-grandfather, a retired lieutenant general, contributed in large part to how I perceived the military community. As the progenitors of the military discipline and structure in my family, these great men showed me the kind of man I wanted to be and I strove to be just as hardworking and self-actuating.

Aside from my personal habits, this dedication to excellence carried over to academics, where I was always near the top of my class. Relying upon self-discipline, I became obsessed with good grades, and to this day, I can still say that I've only ever received one B+ (I missed receiving an A- by .01 percentage point after my teacher lost my last assignment, not that I'm keeping track or anything).

I was equally as devoted to sports as I was to academics. I played both soccer and baseball as a kid, but by the time I reached high school, I had dropped those sports to pick up football, lacrosse, and track. The years and years I spent playing team sports and learning to be part of a group taught me teamwork and cooperation—two skills that have served me quite well in my life so far. Whether it was running the football or sprinting the field in lacrosse, sports taught me to trust other people as well as giving me determination, endurance, and mental strength. Maybe it was because I was angling to become a marine one day, but I always loved contact sports. The constant forceful collisions probably weren't good for my head, but the sports pitted me against myself as well as against other players on the field. I was always working to become better and stronger to make up for my light weight and unintimidating size. I received a few injuries over the years, but I always forced myself to bounce back and get on the field.

Being smaller and younger than other kids in my grade didn't hold me back. I fought and worked to become better. But it was what was going on inside of my heart and mind that truly helped to shape my perspective.

In addition to passion and devotion, my parents had also instilled in me a sense of curiosity and awe about the world around me, leading me to delve into good books. I especially loved the ones with complicated story lines. When I wasn't doing what every other kid my age was doing—riding bikes, playing in the creek, going to the park, building forts, and simply enjoying my childhood—I would become consumed by these books. Reading and studying took my thoughts to other places, and I can adamantly affirm that the hours I spent reading space books are the reason I developed a secondary dream of becoming an astronaut—a dream I still haven't entirely thrown out the window to this day.

I was a Boy Scout and later became an Eagle Scout. So naturally, among other activities, I loved camping and was always the kid the leaders would tell to "put the fire back in the pit." The many hours I spent earning merit badges and the endless backpack hikes I went on "taught me character," as my father would put it. One of those merit badges—first aid—came in handy later on when I was seriously injured in Brussels. That training helped me keep calm in the face of my injuries. So many of the things I learned as a Boy Scout still stick with me. And perhaps most intriguing, it was my experience in Scouts that helped to expand my understanding of and devotion to my faith.

Over the years, I always brought a pocketknife with me when we camped, and I can remember nights out in the cold, dark woods shivering by the fire and whittling sticks as I listened to the grown-ups talk about how God had profoundly changed their lives. As they spoke about their experiences, I would typically stare up at the stars to find a rather dimly lit one. I'd wonder whether there was someone else who was staring back at me twelve billion light-years away, deep in the speckled, black abyss. If there was, I wanted to find that person and prove once and for all that we weren't entirely alone in the universe.

But I wasn't merely lost in the brilliance of the night sky. I was intently listening to and taking in the adults' stories about their personal experiences with the Lord—narratives that had a profound influence on my perspective, leading me to wonder at the power of God to change people. I wondered if He existed and if He could truly reach into my life and make something precious out of it.

It was these simple moments that would prepare me to think deeper about the unseen and to ponder the power of the very Lord who would, years later, save me from wrath and terror. In the moment, though, the conversations forced me to think deeper and ponder harder. And to ask myself some deep questions. Although both my mother and my father were spiritual, religion wasn't forced on me. So often, the faith we come to rely on later in life is shaped in our early years, and this was most certainly the case for me.

Like many kids, I had simply accepted the faith of my parents. I went to church, said my prayers, performed service at church activities, and did every other little thing a practicing Christian would do. I certainly knew deep in my heart that the teachings and beliefs that I was taught at church were good things, and so I lived those standards: respect women, serve others, and do your best to love people, even if they seem different.

Over time, though, I came to realize that the foundation my parents had provided was not only leading me to take actionable steps, but was also deeply transforming my heart and mind. Those good and heartfelt teachings took a hold of my soul and put me on a path to becoming more like Jesus Christ—a journey that I remain on today.

As I matured and entered high school, my perspective continued to widen and develop. I was beginning to understand something that I just hadn't appreciated before. I started to realize that human beings are not all the same. This may seem like an elementary fact to some, but everybody has to learn that at some point. The turning point for me was learning about other cultures in school. I came to realize that humans clearly have some profound cultural and ideological differences. As my teachers opened new doors with information about European history, Middle Eastern writing forms, and African colloquialisms, among other subjects, I began to see the world through a much less rigid lens. While I still couldn't always understand why other people thought the way they did, I was at least slowly beginning to understand the roots of their beliefs and practices.

That process wasn't easy. It's difficult for a person who grew up in a capitalist republic to understand the thought processes of someone raised in a socialist or communist society. But having different experiences—or even starkly disagreeing with an individual or group of people—doesn't mean empathy can't govern our interactions and perceptions. You can't really have true empathy unless you can understand the feelings and thoughts of others, at least to some degree. I had no idea at the time that this was a life lesson that would later resurface during the most harrowing experiences of my life.

I was so enthralled with the different cultures I encountered in my studies that I began creating a visual map in my head to try and encapsulate the finer details of world history. I didn't have the full picture then, nor did I have all of the information, but it was an attempt to more fully understand the world around me. I figured that it would be ignorant of me to reject something simply because I didn't understand it, so I set out on a more specific quest to better comprehend world religions. Rather than taking the effort to embrace all of their teachings, it was my chance to recognize what diverse groups of people believe—and why they believe it.

I remember the first time I learned about the specifics of Catholic Mass. At first, it seemed like the most bizarre thing on planet Earth, as it was entirely different from what I was accustomed to. Yet now that I have a much firmer understanding of organized religion, I can state with some certainty that Mass is actually closer to my own weekly church services than the services that are held by most other religions.

It's incredible how quickly my perception of religion changed once my understanding broadened. Studies of Martin Luther and John Calvin gave me context on the reformation of certain Christian churches, and photos and audio clips of pastors depicted their practices. I investigated Hinduism and the accounts of Rama; I visited a Hindu temple and experienced firsthand how they live their religion. I read theological studies of Buddhism with a pinch of salt, knowing that a theologian doesn't necessarily have the same understanding that a disciple does.

I began seeing parallels of the stories of Horace with events in the life of Jesus Christ and of certain practices during Ramadan with the road to Nirvana. Monotheism and polytheism began to demonstrate their similar values. History books gave me the stage, and technological mediums provided the elements.

I perceived that, in most cases, religions were systems that brought about good. And while there are those who manipulate and even kill others in the name of religion, those people almost always fail to emulate the attributes that their religion teaches. Aside from my own personal preoccupations, I reserve judgment of such individuals to God.

It was after studying religion that I felt the Lord was calling me to take some serious and specific steps in my life.

I considered serving as a volunteer missionary for my church and began receiving specific feelings from God that further encouraged me to take steps in that direction. These feelings, which emitted gently from the core of my being, came as I read holy scripture. Thinking about and practicing the gospel of Jesus Christ gave me peace. Repentance brought me relief. Armed with personal experiences and convictions, I decided to serve as a missionary.

It was a decision that would forever transform my life.

CHAPTER 2 |
Boston |

Darkness cannot drive out darkness; only light can do that. Hate cannot drive out hate; only love can do that.

—Martin Luther King Jr.[2]

I've always admired the colonial city of Boston. Through my studies of history, my interest in Boston was instigated by learning of its role in the American Revolution. I was fascinated by the story of the thousand Puritans seeking political and religious freedom from a tyrannical monarchy and using that thirst for freedom to found what would become the United States of America. I was amazed that their sacrifice and their ideals would cultivate the most powerful nation in the world, a nation that I was privileged to call home.

Because I am an avid sports fan, the sports tradition in Boston also had its appeal. And though it would be a stretch to say I was a fan of any of the New England players, I admired the city's teams nonetheless. The sports alone were enough to make visiting Boston something to look forward to.

Eventually, that opportunity came when my mother was accepted to compete in the Boston Marathon when I was fifteen years old. A great athlete in her own right, my mom's preparation for this historic event inspired me, and her excitement over the chance to take part was absolutely contagious.

The Boston Marathon is known as one of the most prestigious running competitions in the world, with thousands of athletes from around the globe traveling to the United States each year to participate in what is, for many, a once-in-a-lifetime opportunity. Since 1897, Boston has hosted hundreds of thousands of participants who come together to embark on the quest to complete the 26.2-mile journey. It's an event that brings people together in pursuit of a common goal, where people of all backgrounds run side by side and help each other succeed.

The memory of my mother preparing for the marathon reminds me of the many qualities that I admire most about her. Her commitment to never giving up as well as her uncanny ability to teach others to persevere—while upholding the utmost respect and sportsmanship—are some of the most powerful qualities that distinguish this remarkable woman I'm blessed enough to call Mom. And they are qualities that I strive to emulate.

My mother has always been dedicated. As a runner, she has participated in eleven marathons so far (Boston was her eighth). If you were to ask her why she was so intent on running the Boston Marathon, she would say, "It's something every runner aspires to. After several other marathons, it's like icing on the cake." My mom had actually registered for the event in 2012, but she became pregnant with my youngest sister, Tayla, and had to postpone her dream. But one year after her surprise pregnancy, she was out on those rolling Boston roads, running her heart out.

Throughout my many forays into sports, I have found that few athletic events cultivate and display sportsmanship like a marathon. It's not unusual to see runners who drop out of the race—defeated by the heat, cold, injury, or fatigue—and elect to stay and cheer on the runners who remain; others might sometimes sacrifice their own chance at winning to help a fellow runner who is struggling to reach the finish line. There are few athletic events in which simply *finishing* is a commendable cause for celebration.

After all, marathons are events much more profound than exercises in competitive running. They represent something deeply unique, peaceful, and distinctly human, where the finish line serves as more of a victory over an individual's inner self than a triumph over one's fellow man. Either way, a marathon is the culmination of hard work and sacrifice; it's an event where one's dignity and work ethic are on full display—until April 15, 2013, when the Tsarnaev brothers perverted this tradition and marred this noble human endeavor with their ruthless terror attack.

Leading up to the race that day, my parents decided that, since I'm the oldest kid in the family, I'd be able to travel to Boston with them and my grandparents to watch my mom participate in the race of a lifetime. I remember walking around the streets the night before the competition, simply admiring the historic city. The intricate European detail of the mature buildings truly stood out to me. Even attending the Boston Red Sox game in my newly purchased jersey at Fenway Park felt like a tiny bit of paradise.

The Green Monster (the thirty-seven-foot left field wall at Fenway Park) was quite a sight to see. Many Major League Baseball players have expressed both excitement and intimidation over having to go up against the Green Monster, so seeing it in person was quite special. And seeing now-retired Hall-of-Famer David Ortiz in action while everyone in the entire stadium stood in unison and cheered was electrifying.

Mason in front of the Green Monster at a Red Sox game, the day before the bombing.

Following the game, I remember strolling the bustling Boston streets, taking in the delicious aromas of restaurants' and street vendors' food that filled the air. I'm the first to admit that we have great food out West, but there was something to be found in Boston's culinary palate as well.

It was the entire package. The sports, the smells, the chilly breeze, the culture, the people—all were so unfamiliar to me, yet somehow the feelings I had being in Boston that night were collectively akin to being in a familiar place.

The morning of April 15, 2013, soon arrived, and race day was upon us. A unique blend of excitement and anxiety was almost palpable in the early hours of that day, as my mom would soon begin the 26.2-mile journey toward her lifelong goal: completing the grueling marathon.

My dad and I boarded an early metro and made the thirty-five-minute ride out to Heartbreak Hill. The site was a swarm of students from Boston College and fanatical family members, each one looking for friends and loved ones participating in the marathon as an endless chain of people flowed by. One of the first runners I remember passing us was a Navy SEAL; he was in full fatigues and was wearing a pack just as large as him. There were also college track athletes, each one sporting a jersey from their home school. While the pool of participants was diverse, they all shared one feature: a look of determination.

It was a brisk morning with the breeze from the surrounding water making its way through the city. I remember standing at the side of a Boston street, admiring the beauty of the morning and taking in the excitement emanating from the runners and spectators alike. I could just imagine how excited my mom must have been so near to completing such a huge goal. I felt a surge of pride.

The adrenaline from the excitement of it all made me feel as if even I could one day compete in the race. We watched as each runner trudged up Heartbreak Hill to a chorus of hollering bystanders who were voicing encouragement and convincing their friends and loved ones that that they could, in fact, finish the race.

"You can do it!" "Keep going!" and "You've got this!" were just some of the phrases that burst out from the crowd of onlookers. Meanwhile, my dad, being the social butterfly he is, started talking to a bunch of Boston College students, and before I knew it, he had all twenty of them chanting

"Kym, Kym, Kym!" while they searched for my mom, who was sporting a gray top and black shorts.

Five minutes passed, then fifteen. We still hadn't seen her but she could have been going slower than usual. Thirty minutes passed, and then forty. There was still no sign of her. We began to get worried. At fifty minutes, my dad checked the marathon tracker on his phone and realized we had missed her. Understandably, we were upset.

"Let's hurry," my dad said. "We might be able to get to the finish line in time to catch her if we go now." We jumped on the metro and began the thirty-minute ride back to the finish line in hopes of seeing my mom cross it.

When we came out of the metro, it was absolutely packed with people, as there were still endless numbers of people on the sidelines cheering on runners as they finished their last stretch of the race. We began the long trek down Boylston Street toward the finish line on the north side.

Pushing and weaving when we had to, we made our way toward the finish line just before my dad let out a disappointed sigh.

"We missed her by twenty minutes," he said.

"Where is she now?" I asked.

"Somewhere past the finish line," he replied. "The hard part now is finding her."

We continued down Boylston Street and arrived at Exeter Street. But my dad paused for a moment and then uttered some words that very well could have saved our lives that day.

"I feel like we should cross here," he said. "It's going to be a nightmare to get past that finish line right now." Sure enough, it was incredibly loud, and bystanders were packed shoulder to shoulder.

"Okay, let's try not to get hit," I said, and darted across the road alongside him after finding a fleeting opening between runners.

We made our way down Exeter Street about seventy yards and had just rounded the corner onto Blagden Street when we felt and heard an explosion. The noise shattered the sound of city traffic and forced us to immediately stop in our tracks as the windows of the buildings encircling us violently vibrated.

Suddenly, those cheers and happy smiles of victory morphed to expressions of horror and dismay as people realized what had happened

As I stood frozen near Copley Square on Blagden Street near the finish line, I wasn't quite sure what to do, as I nervously took in the scenes around me.

Oh no, the bleachers must have collapsed, I thought.

I whirled around and saw my dad, along with every other person out on road, stopped dead in their tracks as well. We could see debris drifting across the road behind us, and runners between the last fifty to one hundred yards had stopped to gawk at something just out of sight.

The looming skyscraper windows I had been admiring moments earlier reverberated. The movement caused windows closer to the explosion to shatter, the sound drowned out in the roar of the bomb. In that instant, I felt incredibly fragile. Things went eerily quiet as time passed. The silence was absolute as people tried to process what they had heard. The bomb seemed to have sucked all of the sound waves and let them all out in that blast.

"I've lived in Boston for eight years and never heard anything like that," a young man with a black beard and brown backpack told us.

He had barely finished his sentence when a second explosion ripped through the air. This one was farther away, but it completely destroyed the eerie silence that had fallen on the scene in between the two detonations. It was then that screams became very audible.

It wasn't the bleachers, I realized. *It was a bomb.*

Pure turmoil and hell broke loose in the moments that followed as my dad and I watched people flee the scene, not knowing exactly what danger they were running from—or into.

"We need to go!" my dad said, as he grabbed my arm and we joined the crush of others who were fleeing the scene. The two of us took off from Exeter Street and turned, running towards Copley Square. Large numbers of people had begun running from the two sites with stunned looks in their eyes.

"What's going on?" I asked my dad.

"I don't know, but we need to find your mom—now!"

"Where is she? Does her tracker show where she is now?" I asked.

"No," he said. "It stopped when she crossed the line." He released his grip on my arm so we could move more quickly at a jogging pace.

While we knew few details in that moment, it was evident—especially from his stunned reaction—that something was terribly wrong.

I would learn later that not far from where I was, emergency workers were racing back and forth, just as confused and bewildered as the rest of the crowd, sometimes holding people and other times pushing them in wheelchairs or on stretchers.

As we stood on a street corner, the total chaos that had filled the area seemed to briefly abate as people collectively paused to take in all that was happening. The silence that had blanketed the area was suddenly broken by the sound of ambulances rushing to the scene to take the injured to area hospitals.

We ran past Copley Square to see the smoky remains of something I didn't understand. The bleachers were still up, but there was debris around the finish line and commotion with people running back and forth. There were shouts and unidentifiable sounds just out of my line of sight. It made me nervous.

My father and I turned, now running toward Stuart Street. We had moved two blocks away from Copley Square when he turned to me and said, "I'm going to find your mother. Go straight to the hotel and wait for me there, okay?"

He told me to lock the door and stay inside while he searched for her.

"I can help you find mom," I protested.

"No, I want you to go straight to the hotel room and stay there until I come for you, okay?" he said.

I nodded and turned back the way we had come. We were both still unsure of what was going on, but we knew that it wasn't good. Chaos abounded, but I was focused on maneuvering down the sidewalk in front of me, purposefully refusing to look toward the finish line as I passed it for the second time.

Police cars and ambulances appeared out of nowhere, flying around the corner and ignoring painted lines as they barreled toward Copley Square. I remember two young blonde girls who were crossing the road and threw themselves out of the way just in time for an ambulance to fly by at thirty-five miles per hour, missing them by a mere foot.

Other people were running, but the vast majority of people just stopped and stared, most of them out of line of sight of the two bomb sites. I made my way another half block and rushed into our hotel. The hotel employees and concierge personnel had abandoned their posts and were helping people into the lobby and off of the streets, but it was obvious that they were just as lost and panicked as the rest of the crowd. There were patrons in the lobby, but they too looked stunned. Everyone had heard the explosions and were now staring out the front doors, watching the aftermath unfold.

I got into a packed elevator and began the ascent to our thirty-fourth floor apartment room. Several of the people next to me had wide eyes as the elevator moved upward.

"Did you hear that boom?" a man standing next to me asked. "It sounded like it came from the marathon."

"It did, near the finish line," I replied. "There were two of them."

"Were they bombs?" a woman asked worriedly.

I paused, but a boy in the center of the elevator cart slowly nodded, as tears began welling in his eyes. Then he spoke, "I saw them go off—they were definitely bombs."

Everyone in the elevator got really quiet. Then, the boy spoke again, proclaiming, "I hope people are okay."

I looked at the ground. I didn't know what to say, and I hadn't taken much time to think about the people who were injured. To be honest, self-preservation had taken over; I had only been thinking about getting myself away from the carnage. It hit me that *real* people with *real* lives had just been killed and maimed. I couldn't bear to think about it for too long. *These kinds of things don't happen; they shouldn't.*

The elevator got to my floor and I slipped out, nodding toward the others. I couldn't bring myself to speak. The doors closed behind me, and I made my way to our hotel room, fumbling my key before opening the door. Our room had a fantastic view of the city, and I could see a large part of the end of the race down below me—at least, what was left of the race.

I could clearly see the second bomb site from the window. Where there had been crowds of people there were now none, and the sidewalk had been reduced to a trauma center. Several emergency vehicles had pulled up to the blast site and first responders in yellow and black clothes were rushing back and forth, pulling stretchers and moving fences and debris from the area. It was organized pandemonium.

The bottom of the building where the bomb had detonated was littered with glass and other building materials. In the confusion, it was hard to make out what was happening and who was doing what. On the street between me and the site, I could see police vehicles beginning to line up. Soon there was a complete command post. As my eyes moved down the street, I could see ambulances beginning to pile up at the bottom of our hotel. First there were three, then four, then five. Very quickly, the road leading to our hotel entrance became the staging point for ambulances responding to the scene.

I could see clearly from my hotel room window where the second bomb had detonated—and the wreckage and chaos just below me was both mind-blowing and gut-wrenching. Turning away from what was happening below, I turned on the TV, and the news stations were filled with headlines and proclamations such as "Boston Marathon Bombing with Multiple Casualties" and "Terror Strikes Boston."

Not only was I in complete shock experiencing the sights, smells, and aftereffects of the pure hell that these terrorists had wrought below but I was also worried about my mom and her safety. I was worried about my dad lost in the panicked crowds. I was worried that the bombs weren't over, that any moment another blast would rip through the streets, causing more loss of life. Nothing in that moment seemed real. It was as though I was embroiled in the heat of a nightmare, desperately hoping to wake up, realize that it had all simply been a dream, and drift back into a blissful rest.

I took some time to pace the room as I collected my thoughts.

As I walked over to my hotel room window for a second time and once again looked below, I could see the National Guard arriving in armored vehicles, dressed in full duty gear, armed with AR-15s and other weapons and searching the devastated area for those responsible for the attack.

My worry turned to panic as my mind raced with questions about when—and if—my parents would return safely and uninjured. But as I stared off in an intense state of worry, fearing the worst but hoping for the best, my trance was broken by the sound of a text message alert from my dad. He said he had located my mother and that she was safe and uninjured and that they were on their way back to the hotel.

Thank goodness.

My dad went on to explain that my mother had been so excited about finishing the race that she hadn't even heard the blasts at the finish line. She had been confused and lost in the ensuing chaos. But once he located her, Dad grabbed her hand and told her that they needed to leave the area immediately because terrorists had detonated bombs near the finish line.

Despite the horror we had experienced, the text message brought me relief because it confirmed that my mother wasn't injured or killed in the blasts. And while I took immediate solace in that fact, my thoughts went wild as I realized that, though my mother was not injured, a lot of people were soon to experience the reality that their friends and family members wouldn't be coming home; the feeling of joy that I had wouldn't be enjoyed by all.

This was a heartbreaking realization that forced me to stop and immediately pray for all those that were affected by the tragedy. I again peered out the window, looking at the buildings around us and noticing bomb squads on the roof with dogs, aggressively searching for any more signs of terrorism. *Ours is probably next,* I figured.

My continued observations were then interrupted by a call from my dad. I quickly pulled out my phone and answered.

"Are you in the hotel room?" he asked.

"Yes, I'm up here and I'm safe."

"The hotel is going on lockdown, and they're not running the elevators. Can you come down?"

"I'll come right down." I hung up my phone and began the long thirty-four-floor descent back down to the hotel lobby.

There were now several hundred people strewn across the lobby. Firefighters near the doors were attending to an older gentleman who seemed to have collapsed in the panic. Many of the people there were runners, obviously tired and confused. I quickly found my parents in the sea of glittering emergency blankets and ran over to them. I gave my mother a hug and let out a sigh of relief. Over her shoulder, I could see the flat-screen TVs in the hotel lobby, playing a recording of the explosions. I let out another sigh of relief.

I was only fifteen years old at the time, but the event immediately gave me a lens into the fragility of life, showing me that, as humans, we shouldn't take anything for granted. Simply seeing the faces of my mother and father after they had fought their way back to the hotel offered me additional solace. Not only were they safe, but they also offered a sense of familiarity amid a sea of terror and sadness. In that moment, looking into their eyes offered comfort. As shocking as it was, my first exposure to terror was tempered by my proximity to loved ones. Instead of internalizing and harboring the terror, I could share what had happened and get it off my chest. I had family to lean on and really help me process what I had just experienced.

In the hours that passed, our hotel stayed on lockdown. National Guard soldiers were posted at the hotel entrance, and a SWAT team set up a staging area on the street outside. There were still endless sirens but the commotion finally started to decline. We were in that lobby for a long time, watching the news from the TVs that were there and speaking with other people who had witnessed the blasts. At one point, my dad was even interviewed over the phone by CNN. Eventually, the elevators were unlocked, and we made our way up to our room. From there, we watched the rest of the scene from our window.

As day turned to dusk, the police lifted the lockdown on our area for a brief time. In the hour or so that it was lifted, we grabbed our car and drove out of town. There were multiple checkpoints to get out of the area, and I remember seeing military vehicles and wishing that they were away in other countries, not responding to a crisis on our home soil. In my heart, I offered a prayer of gratitude that we had not been injured:

Father, thank you for keeping our family safe, and thank you for allowing my mother to finish her marathon safely. Be with those that are injured tonight as well as their families. Thank you for good people like firefighters and police officers that are here to help. In the name of Jesus Christ, amen.

With that prayer, we drove off into the dark city night.

I was still moved by the heroism I observed as we journeyed back home. I remembered looking down from my hotel window at random strangers running into the blast site to help those in need. Those people were exhibiting Christlike attributes as they cared for the wounded and brought them to safety. If there was ever any sort of silver lining in the wake of the terror I had witnessed, it was this. Evil will attempt every day to unravel us to our core to remove us from the very freedom that we enjoy. Love, however, is a much stronger force than hate, showing the depths of its power when evil attempts to drown out its light.

It doesn't matter where you are, what country you're from, what language you speak, whether you are black or white—the natural human act of love will always rise above and trample evil. Though this was my first experience with terror, it would set the stage and help me process what was to come later. While sharing my story, I don't want to waste too much time discussing the terrorists that committed these horrific acts. Instead, I want to focus on the love and positivity that emerged in the wake of each of their assaults on innocence.

The Boston Marathon bombing challenged my thinking—and my faith—in profound ways. Up to that point, I had heard of horrific tragedies, but reading about an attack or seeing something on the news is quite different from experiencing it. Sure, we all mourn tragedy, but I had always assumed I probably wouldn't ever be personally affected by one—certainly not an attack on the scale of the Boston bombing.

My faith was something that I grew to cherish throughout my life—and for anyone who embraces faith or religion, they know it isn't something that develops overnight; it's something that grows alongside you—a commitment you must invest in if you want to see it expand. I never thought in my wildest dreams that the Boston attack would be the start of a series of heartbreaking events in my life—incidents that would attempt to take from me the joy that faith brings to my life. We are all often challenged in extreme ways, but I never entertained the notion that terror would be amid those challenges in my life.

In the wake of Boston, I saw my studies of world history differently. I came to see things from a bigger and broader perspective. Some of the gray in the world suddenly lightened up for me after the attacks, and I began to be more conscious of my own actions as a person. I spent more time thinking about the world beyond my immediate life, and my scripture study took on a sense of urgency as I attempted to learn the answers to some truly difficult questions.

Why would God allow bad things to happen to His children? Why is life unjust? Where, in fact, is justice? Who are we to decide how justice must be served? What can I do amid such troubling events? I asked these questions over and over, but the answers weren't easily attained; I had to turn to God again and again. And He gave me a hopeful lens through which to recollect the events of that fateful day.

I quickly learned that God's love can be exemplified and lived out through all of us. I have kept that very valuable lesson with me every single day since the Boston attack. There's a well-known quote from the late kids' TV show host Mr. Rogers that truly encapsulates my feelings about what I experienced in Boston:

> When I was a boy and I would see scary things in the news, my mother would say to me "Look for the helpers, you will always find people who are helping." To this day, especially in times of "disaster," I remember my mother's words, and I am always comforted by realizing that there are still so many helpers—so many caring people in this world.[3]

This quote offers an accurate and truthful lesson for us all. It's a pointed reminder that we can combat evil acts of hatred and injustice by doing just the opposite—loving more ceaselessly and fervently.

I also learned, though, that in addition to combating evil and looking for the silver lining, there's a deep power that we retain and exhibit in how we respond to pain and tragedy. Consider Jeffrey Bauman—one of the victims who went viral in the wake of the Boston Marathon attack. He lost both his legs in the bombings, yet has remained intensely positive throughout the ordeal—even with the realization that his life will never be the same. Instead of focusing on the terrorists responsible and focusing on evil, I remember hearing Bauman, when he appeared on TV, thank everyone who had taken him to safety. He said, "Bad people are rare. Good people are everywhere."[4] Those words became a staple for me as I personally continued to process what happened in Boston.

Rather than obsess over his identification as a victim, Bauman simply kept his determination to recover and stayed positive and has, in turn, inspired millions. It just goes to show that we shouldn't focus on the cowardly acts these terrorists commit. After all, that's exactly what they would want. Instead, we need to focus on loving others and staying positive in times of extreme trial and tribulation. If we muster the power to stay strong and come together in times of intense fear and heartache, we can help dismantle the very evil that attempts to rob of us our dignity and happiness.

"Love will make us stronger" was a popular phrase during candlelight vigils that unfolded in the week that followed the Boston attack. As hard as it is to live out that idea, I know firsthand that the concept works when put into practice. Another lesson I took away from the attack is the importance in relying on God's love to help us through horrific—or even difficult—events.

Four years after the attack, Boston is still a city that is very near and dear to my heart. I'm still intensely moved by all I witnessed that day, particularly the brave Bostonians and tourists who ran to help the injured and strangers in need, not caring if they, themselves, were sprinting right into harm's way. The bombings somehow left me feeling an unwavering bond with the city of Boston, as if a piece of my heart and soul were left there.

The saying "Boston Strong" was embraced on social media, T-shirts, and news stations in the wake of the terror attack—and I can't think of anything more fitting because it encompasses the miraculous way that people rallied together to overcome such an evil act of hatred and violence.

I witnessed what "Boston Strong" looked like with my own eyes, and I'm a better and stronger person because of it.

In the end, I do know that we are tested, and if we love and rely on God in all things, we can overcome the obstacles and challenges that come our way.

CHAPTER 3 |
My Navy Calling |

Obstacles don't have to stop you. If you run into a wall, don't turn around and give up. Figure out how to climb it, go through it, or work around it.

—Michael Jordan[5]

When I was eight, I used to hide in the bushes while I waited for my grandparents to visit. If you would have peered through the prickly evergreens, you'd have seen a determined little kid crouching down with a serious face behind a set of green and brown military fatigues. I'd wear a camouflage hat, a fake plastic gun that resembled a rifle by my side. Peering through a cheap pair of binoculars, I would scout out the street from my strategic position on the left side of our front yard, just waiting for the moment my grandparents' car would wind around the bend.

When people passed on the sidewalk, I would crouch and sit motionless, as quiet as a mouse, as they unsuspectingly passed my position. *They don't even know I'm here*, I would tell myself. Whether or not I was as expertly hidden as I believed myself to be, I was convinced I was, and there's no joy quite like that for a little kid playing army.

I would lie in wait for what seemed like hours until their silver car would finally pull around the corner. "It's them!" I would pull my binoculars back up to my eyes and track their car as it came closer. *3 . . . 2 . . . 1 . . . now!* I would jump from the bushes just as their car pulled up to the curb. If I had a smoke bomb, I would throw it out onto the road.

"Hands up! Hands up!" I yelled, as loud as a kid my age could.

"All right, sir! Yes, sir!" they would say as they stumbled out of the car, playing along as smiles stretched across their faces. Eventually hands held high would turn into hugs and I would take them inside. Sure, the entire charade was just that—a charade. The imagination of a child. But even my play as a child was influenced by my deep-seated desire to serve in the military.

Ever since I was young, I dreamed of being a marine. It runs in the family; it's in my blood—my grandfather is a retired colonel in the US Marines, and my great-grandfather was a retired three-star general, a marine to his very core. It's no wonder, then, that I grew up wearing camouflage uniforms and playing with GI Joes. For every Halloween that I can ever remember, I dressed up as a marine, and my parents could never quite convince me to try out a different costume. I not only wanted to join the military; I absolutely *knew* I would be a marine someday. After all, somebody had to protect civility and our way of life, and, in my mind and heart, I felt that would be me. Someday, at least. Until then, I would just keep on dreaming.

Over time, my reasons for wanting to join the military developed and matured. When I was young, the bright sight of explosions and visions of heroism attracted me to the job. I had seen my fair share of old war movies featuring men dressed in marine blues as they stormed beaches and fought in the Pacific. My great-grandfather had been among those Marines. As a captain in World War II, he waded up the volcanic, sandy beaches of Iwo Jima and fought against the Japanese on the rocky steps of Mount Sarabachi. He was a war hero and a stalwart example of character in any sense of the word. He was one of my personal heroes.

But as I grew older and learned more about the US Armed Forces, I began to also see the military in a broader light: as a force for good in the world. I never had to look further than my grandfather to see the type of good men that the Marines made. I knew that the Marines could make me a better person, and I felt as though it was a pathway to something bigger. As I aged, though, I was able to see just how deep these themes ran. The discipline, the rigorous lifestyle—always pushing yourself to the limit—that's what I wanted. I knew that there was evil in the world, and good men needed to thwart it. I felt the call, and I knew in my heart that I could do it.

I first heard about the US Naval Academy in Annapolis, Maryland, as a twelve-year-old in junior high school. My mom had just finished telling me about West Point, and I was excited to hear that there was an equivalent for the US Navy and Marines. (In reality, the Naval Academy is better than West Point, but that's beside the point.) I wanted to become a marine officer, and the Naval Academy would give me the chance to do just that. At the time, of course, I didn't know that they had an 8 percent acceptance rate and that it was more competitive than almost any Ivy League school in the country. At that age, none of that mattered; I was determined. I made up my mind back then that I would be a Naval Academy Midshipman, and I've never really looked back since.

As I went through junior high and high school, I set my course in motion with the waypoint on the Naval Academy. I learned what it took to get in: good grades, outstanding citizenship, leadership and athletic experience, and a host of other qualifying factors. So, I set myself up to take the hardest academic classes that I could and dedicated myself to sports. With time, I knew I could—and would—eventually obtain my goals.

When I was thirteen, my parents took me to the Hill Air Force Base Show, an air show that takes place near my hometown in Utah every two years. I used to look up in profound bewilderment as Air Force bombers, F-16s, F-18s, and stunt planes swirled in the sky above me. As we were leaving that year, my parents bought me a poster that still hangs in my room. It has a picture of the navy's F-18 Blue Angels squadron, a show team that goes around the world to showcase the prowess of the US military, and underneath it reads:

"The tragedy in life does not lie in not achieving your goals. The tragedy lies in having no goals to reach."

I took that to heart, and forming and holding clear goals became a part of who I was. I looked forward to the next ten years and envisioned myself as a marine pilot, flying the globe and doing my part to make the world a safer place—though I never imagined I would face the horror of explosions well before I ever became a soldier.

High school came and not much had changed: I was still set on attending the Naval Academy and becoming an officer. I was performing well in my classes and, on a broader level, doing my best to become a well-rounded person. I ran for student office and became a student body officer (SBO) my junior year. Becoming an SBO taught me a lot about personal responsibility and collaborating with others to achieve a common purpose. I was the youngest SBO in our school, but I learned the value of service and did my best to master the tasks in front of me, seeing the opportunity as another chance to refine my perspective.

During the summer between my junior and senior years, I attended the Naval Academy's Summer Seminar, or NASS as it's commonly referred to (the military loves acronyms). I flew out to Annapolis, Maryland, and was thrust into the world of a Naval Midshipman. The seven-day seminar was more of a test than anything else. As a candidate for the academy, I did my best to understand the lifestyle and perform well.

We were up at 6:30 a.m. for physical training, we attended classes and performed tasks during the day, and marched in the evening. We were yelled at, had water splashed in our faces, and bear crawled far more than I would have liked, but I loved it nonetheless. It was my first taste of a hyper-disciplined life, and I thrived on the associated challenges. It was there that I solidified without a shred of doubt that it was something I truly wanted. I came home for the rest of the summer, but I couldn't share the thrilling experience.

During my seasonal football practices, my mind was running in the distance as I envisioned myself jogging the docks of the Naval Academy and looking out over the Atlantic. At other times, I recalled the fear I experienced at the Boston bombing, as the memories of what happened at the race earlier that year flashed before me. I had witnessed terrorism and evil firsthand. I had seen the panic, anger, and pain that came at the hands of evil men bent on destruction. Those dark memories were in sharp contrast to the positive energy and sense of commitment I felt when I was at the academy, and the latter surely eclipsed the former in my mind. The academy became engraved in my heart and soul as an institution that pushed good—the very good that was needed to defeat the flagrant evil I witnessed in Boston.

As my schooling progressed, I kept my grades up and kept my eye on the prize ahead of me. All the while, my understanding of God and goodness was evolving. I saw parallels between the virtues of honesty, integrity, and service that the Naval Academy instilled and the doctrine that Jesus taught. Jesus taught men to love God, and the academy taught men to love country. "Greater love hath no man than this, that a man lay down his life for his friends," Jesus taught in John 15:13 (KJV). The military embodied that teaching through action.

My increasing efforts to reach my academic and professional goals came at the same time that my faith progressed. And there was a clear difference in my life as I more intensely practiced and applied the teachings of the man they called Jesus of Nazareth. I found that I was happier and more at peace during the turbulent times of my life. Adversity began to bear a reason, and I found that prayer opened my heart to a better understanding of who I was and why I was here. My belief that all good things are gifts from God led me to a profound gratitude and respect for the principle of freedom—a sentiment that I believe would have deeply resonated with the Founding Fathers. That belief strengthened my resolve to serve in the US military, and my faith grew hand in hand with my sense of purpose.

In the fall of 2013, while most high school seniors were settling in to their last year of school, I was finishing up my application to both the Air Force Academy and the Naval Academy. As I began meeting with the staff of senators and congressmen to obtain a nomination to each, my mind was also drawn to the possibility of a third option for my immediate future: missionary work.

Young men and women of my faith have the opportunity, if they so desire, to serve a mission at the age of eighteen or nineteen. Missionaries are assigned to a specific area of the world where they live, learn the language, and share the teachings of Jesus Christ with other people, whether they be strangers or otherwise. A mission lasts two years, and from a young age I had committed myself to one day go out and share what I had learned about my faith with other people. The possibility of a mission was clear in my head as I continued my academy applications.

By the time April 2014 came, I had passed the medical and physical portions of the Naval Academy application, but was still waiting to hear as to whether I would be accepted into that incredible institution. I remember April 1 of that year as if it were yesterday.

I had been at work and was headed home after a long day of school and unloading boxes in a warehouse. I got to my house and walked through the garage door to find my parents with heavy looks on their faces; my mother was crying. They pulled me aside and told me the devastating news: I had been rejected from the US Naval Academy.

Upon hearing the news, everything in my mind came to a grinding halt. I didn't even process it the first time I heard it.

"You didn't make it," my mother repeated a second time. "We just got the call."

I stood there for a moment, motionless and calm. In a flash, I grabbed my keys and barreled back out the garage door. I drove to a plateau that overlooked our valley and shook my hands toward God in the encroaching snowstorm.

"How could this happen? How could you do this to me?" I asked, with anger overtaking me. My pacing was unrelenting as the snow storm worsened, heavy flakes blazing through the freezing air.

Then, I unleashed a flurry of proclamations and questions: "This is everything I've worked toward in life! You know what this means to me! I thought that this was what you wanted. I felt so good about it! I've always thought that this was a path that you would bless me on. Why this? Was I wrong? Was all of this in vain?"

I continued to pace and gripe to God as the wet snow accumulated inside the park. I knew that God always knew best, but I couldn't bring myself to accept that *this was best*, that *this was happening.*

My dream is dead, I thought. *All of that was for nothing.*

Only now, looking back, is it obvious that it wasn't for nothing—there was a grander plan.

What I couldn't see in those desperate moments was that in trying to make myself fit for acceptance into the Naval Academy, I had molded my character and made myself more than I could have ever been without setting those goals. Despite the disappointment that consumed me that day, I eventually came to understand that falling short of the goals of yesterday didn't prevent me from aspiring to new things tomorrow.

The next day, I realized, was the first day of the rest of my life, and if I wanted to make that life great, I had to choose to have a positive perspective. The part of me that had grown and persevered as a result of my efforts was still with me and would catapult me toward other God-ordained successes.

I quickly realized that, no matter what, I needed to keep moving forward. As I prayed to God that night, the path in front of me was illuminated. The next day, I found myself in my bishop's office, preparing to serve as a missionary. At the end of my senior year, I was called to serve for two years in Paris, France. Upon learning the news, I was ecstatic. I had taken French in high school and was anxious to immerse myself in what was a relatively foreign world.

Mason and his parents on the day of his mission call to France.

CHAPTER 4
Paris

*We do not learn from experience. We
learn from reflecting on experience.*
—John Dewey[6]

A portion of my innocence was shattered during the Boston
bombing, and though my faith recovered in the following
years, I had no idea that it was merely the beginning of
a long and complicated journey. My next encounter with
terror came two years after Boston while I was serving a
mission in Rouen, France.

I arrived in Rouen in October 2014 and was stationed
about eighty miles from Paris—a city I visited fairly fre-
quently. And about two weeks before deadly terror attacks
struck on November 15, 2015, I observed firsthand some of
the unrest that had been percolating under the surface of the
country.

Mason at the Porte Serpenoise during his mission in France.

It was just weeks before, on October 31, when my missionary companion and I took a tram to the middle of Rouen. The heart of the city is laced with timeless cobblestone streets and centuries-old buildings. It all flows into one of the most traveled streets by pedestrians in Europe, the Rue du Gros-Horloge. This street is rather narrow, with most cars typically not daring to use it because of all the people that tend to frequent it.

As we passed under the Gros-Horloge—a gigantic clock adorned in gold that dates back to 1889—we came upon a police van. The van was for the Compagnies Républicaines de Sécurité, or, more plainly stated: the riot police.

These police are infamous for taking down looters and breaking up riots (including the not-so-rare riots after soccer games). They are prevalent all throughout France, and if you see them it is usually a sign that you should probably be somewhere else. It took us a second to realize that along with six or seven police vans, we were the only people out on this road. It was about 7:30 p.m., and there wasn't a soul out on the streets.

The vans were stationed in a single-file line and they were slowly inching down the middle of the street. As we walked up behind them, we started to notice a startling scene all around us—virtually every store on the road had been vandalized. We peered inside the vans as we passed them; each one had eight or so riot shield police armed to the teeth with angry and determined looks on their faces. I figured they were unhappy because the vans were uncomfortable, but I'd soon discover that there was much more to the story.

As we rounded the corner, the air was suddenly hit with a maelstrom of angry chants in Arabic. We saw hundreds of figures, all of them dressed in black with white masks on their faces. They were throwing flares out onto the road and at the windows of commercial stores. They were tagging everything from columns to benches with spray paint. I didn't understand the symbol they kept painting—it was foreign to me. The group was protesting a recent intervention in Palestine by the French.

Several of the figures in the back of the horde saw us and pointed to us. They started yelling angrily in French. At that point, we had seen enough and promptly ducked off the street toward the cathedral, leaving the commotion behind us.

———

Weeks later, I witnessed a gathering of a much different type. When the Charlie Hebdo attack happened in January 2015, France was stunned. People couldn't comprehend a tragedy like that on their own soil, even given past attacks that had unfolded. After the killing of twelve people at the offices of the satirical magazine, the collective societal pain in France was palpable.

I remember the candlelight vigil that was held on Rouen that same night. Locals who donned black clothing walked slowly down the city's main streets. There were thousands of them steadily pouring through the square in a stunning procession of mourning. Despite the somber demeanor, their candles collectively glittered like moonlight off the waves of a calm evening sea.

Here we were, two young men in white shirts, overcome by the reverential procession that stretched out in front of us. As we fissured slowly through the crowd, we looked at the faces of the people around us; they were solemn. We left the scene behind us, and the only thing I could think about was how horrible the families of the victims must have felt.

I reflected on these very elements in a missionary journal I kept throughout my time abroad, noting that—in addition to mourning—there was additional strife unfolding inside France at the time:

Journal Day 144:

Things for the rest of France are not super great right now. There [have] been 4 shootings in the last 3 days. The first one was in Paris and 11 died. The other 3 were instances where cops were killed. Needless to say, the people are riled up and pitted, French against Muslims (and religion in general). That's not good for us—there's literally a mosque right out back of our apartment. There was a big manifestation in Rouen today and the day before. Me and Christensen walked straight through the middle of one the other day, not knowing what it was.

But the anguish that followed the Charlie Hebdo attack was only the beginning of the trauma that would befall France during our time there. Months later, France would once again experience that horror, with terrorists wreaking havoc throughout the city of Paris in November 2015, killing 130 and wounding hundreds of others. Though I was miles away in Calais at the time, it was yet another event that hit far too close to home—one that left me contemplating how to process the hate and fear that I seemingly couldn't evade.

It was an early morning for my companion, Elder Jouffray, and me. We were out performing some service for members of our congregation and were wrapped up in our usual missionary affairs that we had grown accustomed to while abroad. I'll never forget where we were when we found out what was happening.

Elder Jouffray and I were working on a computer at our church, ordering some train tickets when we received a cryptic text message from our mission president.

"The mission is on lockdown," it read.

Lockdowns weren't completely foreign to us as missionaries. Every now and then, the missionaries in various cities would be advised to stay indoors if something dangerous was happening; in fact, we had gone on lockdown earlier that year during the Charlie Hebdo shooting. Naturally, upon receiving the text, my companion and I quickly switched our computer screen from the train booking website to a French news outlet, and sure enough, on the front page, we saw that terrorists had tragically struck France once again. I could feel a deep, visceral pain in the pit of my stomach that was birthed from intense emotion. Once again, the blight of terrorism had emerged—and with a tragic and deadly vengeance.

A flurry of emotions ran through the French populace that cold November morning. Many were left shocked, angry, and destitute, trying to process all that had unfolded. Traumatic and stirring events like that tended to lead the people toward cynicism. It's difficult to understand something so simultaneously horrific and confusing—something so far out of the reach of our immediate lives. But unfortunately, violence, death, and destruction had struck the French, and the results were heartbreaking. The violence that these terrorists inflicted tainted the atmosphere. Amid the resulting pain, I absolutely understood why some people were hardened in their hearts. I had myself been somewhat hardened.

And, as a result, it was easy to develop the mentality of some of my French associates, though I was impressed by those who were able to truly live out the concept of turning the other cheek, opening up their hearts to give humanity a second chance. So often I was asked, "How could there be a God, given all the evil in this world?" It's a question every human being asks him or herself at least once (and for many, it's a curiosity that repeatedly edges its way into the human psyche).

Either way, it's never an easy topic to explore or settle on because the problem of human pain has plagued generations since Adam, gnawing at peoples' hearts and minds. In the Old Testament, Job, perhaps, gives us the best lens into how humanity attempts to explore these issues; it's a timeless story that some might see as a mirror that reflects some of the same struggles we all have. Here's how a *Psychology Today* article once explained the epic biblical book:

> The story of a good man named Job challenges the guilt/suffering paradigm by illustrating that even the most righteous suffer. If suffering is a punishment of sorts, then why should the righteous, who by definition are without (much) sin, be afflicted with trauma?
>
> The overarching theme of The Book of Job examines the injustice of traumatic suffering; and the aridity of simplistic explanations.[7]

Thousands of years after the book's writing, Job's own pleas offer us a robust look at the human condition:

> What is mankind that you make so much of them, that you give them so much attention,
>
> That you examine them every morning and test them every moment?
>
> Will you never look away from me, or let me alone even for an instant?
>
> If I have sinned, what have I done to you, you who see everything we do? Why have you made me your target? Have I become a burden to you?
>
> Why do you not pardon my offenses and forgive my sins? For I will soon lie down in the dust; you will search for me, but I will be no more. (Job 7:17–21, NIV)

The question of human pain is truly timeless. In my own experience, the impressions and promptings I have received from God have led me to believe that He allows bad things to happen so that we can become more like Him. For me, it happened through understanding, and it gave me the chance to make choices that have made me a stronger and more grounded person. It's no doubt hard to understand why some of these bad things happen—and why God allows them. And it would certainly be easy to turn bitter and doubt my faith. However, throughout my struggles, I chose to rely heavily on my faith in the Almighty, knowing that God would guide me through any situation imaginable.

But as I sat miles away from Paris on the night of the attack and once again pondered these questions, relying on my faith to process it all, I had no idea that what was about to come next would test my character, resolve, and capacity for forgiveness; what awaited me was a chaos and pain unlike anything I had experienced.

During the weeks following the Paris attacks, we took time out of our zone conferences to review emergency and lockdown procedures. As a missionary in Calais, we faced additional concerns that were unique to our area, mainly an influx of Syrian refugees. Calais sits on the northern tip of France, just across the English Channel from Great Britain. In fact, on a clear day, we could see England from the beach. Calais is home to the Eurotunnel, an underground railroad that connects the two countries and allows for commercial and industrial high-speed trains to pass underneath. When I arrived in Calais in the middle of 2016, there were just over two thousand Syrian refugees living there. By the time of the Paris attacks, there were over eight thousand emigrants living in the northeast quadrant of the city nicknamed "The Jungle."

They were destitute. Initially there were just men, but within a number of months, there were families and children alongside them. Certain sections of the city became dangerous, and we found ourselves trailed several times by refugees who didn't have the best of intentions. When it was rumored that one of the Paris attack plotters was seeking refuge in the city, the police force grew considerably. There were many good people among those refugees, but there were also some bad ones. All the while, I kept my head on my shoulders, as we missionaries did our best to continue our work.

A few months after the Paris attack, I was transferred to Brussels, Belgium, where I once again encountered terrorism, this time inside the city's airport and on a much deeper and more profound level.

CHAPTER 5 |
Seeds of Chaos |

Be strong and courageous. Do not be afraid or terrified because of them, for the Lord your God goes with you; he will never leave you nor forsake you.

(Deuteronomy 31:6, NIV)

March 21, 2016, was a completely ordinary day for me and my seasoned missionary team.

We endured a long conference call early in the day, emailed our families for a few hours, and if my memory serves me right we also picked up some delicious waffles—you know, nothing too extravagant or uncommon. And certainly no sense that this day and the day after would be anything other than ordinary. There were no signs of impending doom, no whispers of anything looming on the horizon. It was just another lovely day in Brussels.

For the most part, I loved my time in Brussels. Our missionary team had truly come to respect and enjoy the city. The entire community in which we served was a unique melting pot of resilient African immigrants, courageous Arab pioneers, intelligent French nationals, and cheerful Belgian citizens.

The cobblestone pathways, the eight-hundred-year-old arches, the specialized artisan shops—these were just some of the things that made Europe a mysterious paradise that we had the privilege to serve in. But although we were distracted by the wonderful scenery and the thought-provoking discussions, we still sometimes missed home, finding ourselves occasionally pining for the familiar.

I often think back to the countless times before the bombings that I entered kebab shops in Brussels to try and find cheap meals and soft drinks. Sometimes, American music would come on and certain songs would instantly take me back to my home out west, and for a moment—just a small, fleeting moment—it seemed like time stood still. Those brief bits of nostalgia would typically end when the cook would belt out our names and shatter our daydreams to let us know that our food was ready.

The music was a connection point to home and the familiar. Often the reality on the ground would also jolt us into remembering that we were essentially strangers in a foreign country where only half of the people could correctly pronounce our names. Overall, we didn't mind it, though (and, in fairness, our French was far worse than their English). In the end, the reality was quite simple: we were foreigners

Mason and Elder Empey on their mission
in Brussels before the attack.

who had set out to share and exercise our faith in a truly unfamiliar place.

The high-speed trains, the tiny taxis, the nonstop trams—each one of these things was a constant reminder that I was in an unfamiliar environment. It wasn't a bad place, or even a violent place. It was just a very different place. And "different" can be scary at first, although I came to learn along the way that new experiences often build character and resolve, even if those experiences have a negative impact on us.

I was young and inexperienced but also passionate and curious. I had found ultimate truth, and I was on a quest to share it with whoever was willing to talk to me. My fellow missionaries and I spoke with anyone who embraced any religion or worldview, exchanging our beliefs with a variety of people along the way.

During our time in Brussels, we entered plenty of peoples' homes and dined with them and their families. We talked about politics on the metro and discussed issues pertaining to social reform on the bus. We routinely listened to many passionate diatribes about how society had turned for the worse—and we even nodded in agreement when it was appropriate to do so, though I didn't always agree with what was being said.

I suppose my point in sharing these experiences is this: Brussels wasn't simply a location where my fellow missionaries and I were placed to fulfill a static mission. We had come to absolutely love the people, places, and things within its confines—and that love had only grown through our diverse experiences and interactions. And it was those elements that shaped our connection to the city, making the devastating events of March 22 that much more soul-crushing.

What started as a simple trip to the airport to drop off a friend devolved into one of the most harrowing experiences of my life.

Six days before the attack, Elder Joseph Empey and I had taken a fellow missionary to the airport, helping us to become well-acquainted with traveling to and from the travel hub. So, when it came time to take Sister Fanny Clain, another missionary, to catch her flight, we had a good idea of what we needed to do to get her there on time.

With that in mind, the morning of March 22 started like any other. The familiar, uncomfortable ring of my alarm went off at 6:30 a.m. Sometimes, getting up was the most difficult part of the day. Refusing to give in to my low energy and morning grogginess, I popped out of bed and offered a morning prayer on my knees. Feeling half-awake, I woke up the other half of my body by rubbing my eyes and pumping out a few push-ups.

Despite my slow start, we were out the door early that day. We snagged a 7:00 a.m. metro at our stop in Koekelberg and made our way out to a train station

Mason and Elder Empey at the metro station the day before the bombing.

toward the middle of the city. It was just early enough for us on the metro to beat the morning business commute in Brussels. Elder Empey received a text from Elder Norby, a senior missionary, and turned to me, saying, "Norby said he's going to pick us up out near the metro stop Schumann."

"When will he be there?" I asked.

"Fifteen minutes or so."

"We should be good to make our train to Namur after we drop off Sister Clain," I replied.

"I think we might need to hurry," he added.

Elder Empey was one of the best companions I had on my mission. Always a go-getter, he never slowed down for anyone and was fearless when it came to talking to people. I first met him in a city named Metz about one year earlier into my mission. There, in a beautiful city on the eastern side of France, we were assigned to work for the same congregation. At the time, I was paired with a different missionary, as was Empey, but we shared the same apartment.

Our apartment was in the center of the city, and it gave us a chance each day to experience the beautiful French and German architecture that dominated the city. During World War I and World War II, Metz was in the heart of the German-French conflict. Considering the complex history, the city switched countries a few times—and every time the Germans or the French reacquired the city, they would immediately begin to build architecture to surpass the engineering of the opposing side.

The result was a city with two identities—a truly beautiful sight to see.

Brussels presented a stark contrast to the bright city we had lived in on the Eastern side of France. Brussels was in Belgium, and was at least four times the size of Metz; it is the home of both the European Union and a large urban sprawl that encompassed two languages, French and Dutch. By the time Elder Empey and I had become companions, we were both a little older and a little wiser. We spoke fluent French and had a handle on how to conduct missionary work.

By the time we were in Brussels, we were zone leaders, and were tasked with overseeing the operations of our mission in Belgium. Taking missionaries to the airport in Brussels was one of our responsibilities and, thus, we found ourselves on the metro early that morning to pick up Sister Clain to take her to her flight home.

We arrived at our stop, and as the doors to the metro opened, the familiar metro voice came over the intercom: "You have arrived at Gare Centrale." Empey rushed out in front me as I trailed behind. We walked into the central hub of the Gare and I got my bearings. It was the first time I had ever been to Gare Centrale, and the marble pillars and glass ceiling were a beautiful distraction.

Empey turned to me, "We need to find her train, do you see it on the screen?"

"I don't, no," I replied.

"Let's go find her rail number."

"If you want to walk down the hub and look at the lines I'll wait here and keep an eye out for her," I added.

I watched Elder Empey rush down the hub, glancing at the rail line monitors as he passed to identify which train was which. He had almost finished walking down one side of the hub when I heard a familiar voice to my left.

"*Salut*, Elder Wells."

I turned to find Sister Clain managing two large suitcases with her small five-foot-three frame. Her train had come in from the city of Liege, which was to my immediate left. I moved towards her and grabbed the bigger suitcase.

"Sister Clain! How was your train ride over?"

"Oh, it wasn't too bad," she replied. "Getting up early wasn't very fun though." I could relate.

Elder Empey came up behind us, "Sister Clain! How are you? Are you excited to fly to the US?"

"Yes, very happy," she replied.

Elder Empey grabbed her other suitcase, and the three of us made our way back to the metro. As the metro approached and the doors opened, we awkwardly lifted her heavy suitcases into the metro car. There were only a few stops between the train station and the Schumann stop where Elder Norby would pick us up.

We got off the metro at Schumann and made our way above ground. Sure enough, Elder Norby was waiting for us just above on the road, with his signature warm smile we were so used to. He waved us over.

"Sister Clain! It's so great to see you! How have you been over in Liege?" he said.

The four of us began to talk and banter as Elder Norby pulled away from Schumann. Little did we know that two hours later a bomb would rip through that very same station, killing almost everyone that was in that metro car.

The drive to the airport was only ten minutes. We really appreciated Elder Norby's offer to drive us because the metro would have taken an additional half hour. If we had taken the metro that day, I'm not sure I'd be writing this. As it was, we arrived at the airport and parked in the parking garage directly adjacent to the terminal and walked in.

I can vividly recall how the airport looked that day. It consisted of one large check-in terminal, a security checkpoint, and then the building branched off in several directions to accommodate the various airlines. The front of the entrance terminal was mostly glass, and a wide sidewalk ran along that portion of the airport, with a two-lane road on the other side of the sidewalk guardrail, which is where people were dropped off.

The four of us walked past the sliding glass doors into the airport and directly towards the Delta check-in. Off to the side were rows of Delta kiosks swamped with passengers trying to print out their tickets.

We walked up to the shortest kiosk line and waited to print Sister Clain's ticket. Because male missionaries always wear a white shirt, tie, and black name tag, this sometimes gave people the false impression that we worked at whatever store or location we were in. And sure enough, a tourist turned to us and said, "I'm having a hard time getting my ticket."

She held out her passport to Elder Empey, who said—without letting her know he wasn't an airport employee—"I can help you out." After all, he was a kind guy and this certainly wasn't his first time dropping off a missionary at the Brussels Airport.

He placed her passport under the kiosk camera and a small *ding* sounded as her information came up on screen.

"Thank you, young man," she said as she printed off her ticket.

Elder Empey smiled. "No problem."

Over the next few minutes, we helped another tourist as well until Sister Clain finally made it to the front of the line. Elder Empey held her passport under the camera, but the kiosk didn't *ding* and didn't pull up her information. He waved her passport under the camera a second time, but again the machine failed to read it.

I knew that we had bought the ticket, because I was holding Sister Clain's ticket confirmation in my hand. I looked over at Elder Empey, who handed me the passport. "I'll try," I said.

After two more unsuccessful attempts on my part, an actual Delta employee came over to us.

"Having trouble?" she asked.

"Yes, our friend's passport won't read on the kiosk machine."

She took the passport and unsuccessfully tried to put it under the camera. She turned back to us and said, "Why don't you try another kiosk?"

After another three-minute wait in line and several more unsuccessful attempts on the second kiosk, she turned again to us and said, "Well, you have to check-in your friend's suitcases anyway. Why don't you just tell the worker at the check-in desk what happened, and he can print off your ticket over there."

We thanked her and walked to the back of the check-in line.

The four of us were in line for thirty seconds when a bomb detonated toward the front of the line. In a fraction of a second, my world erupted.

CHAPTER 6 |
Brussels |

Survival can be summed up in three words: NEVER GIVE UP. That's the heart of it really. Just keep trying.

—Bear Grylls[8]

In an instant, chaos replaced the pale calmness of the scene. An enormous flash of white light burst through the airport. The light was so intense I instinctively squeezed my eyes shut against the visual onslaught. Almost simultaneously, a thunderous boom shattered the stillness, rendering me completely deaf. This all happened in the first half-second following the detonation. Once I was able to open my eyes, maybe a second later, I saw fire raging in front of my face. Everything was still incredibly bright, yet I could only see a few feet in front of me because of vast amounts of floating debris still settling after the detonation. The fire was everywhere, and a horrible pain pulsated throughout my entire body.

For a second, I didn't even feel like I was on my feet at all. The entire right side of my body fluctuated from feeling intensely hot to overwhelmingly cold.

The explosion had torn through the Delta line, peppering the four of us with shrapnel and debris. I looked around me; I was alone in the line. My friends had been blown away by the force of the explosion. The people in front of me in line were similarly absent. I was the only one in the line that was left standing. I looked down. My iPad had been tossed from my hands, my watch had been blown off my wrist, my left shoe was no longer on my foot. The clothes I was wearing were reduced to tattered shreds. All of this happened in less than a second. It was so fast that it was hard to process.

Looking back, my first thought was kind of strange. *This shouldn't be happening in an airport.* My second thought was, *This was a bomb.*

I was disoriented, and in the moment, I was almost sure I had died. I didn't feel anything, the intense shock had temporarily numbed the pain pulsating through my entire body, where before it had burned hottest at my head, hand, and foot on the left side. But as smoke began to fill the room, my senses sharpened and I began to reorient. Then, like I was in a movie, the smoke parted to reveal a horrifying scene—one that has etched itself into my memory.

The first things I saw were dark figures lying on the ground all around me. My head was spinning, and I was struggling to make sense of what I was seeing. I strained my eyes to see past the bodies on the floor. I could see light pouring in from the entrance doors of the airport, though the doors themselves had been completely blown out. Shattered pieces of glass littered the ground.

It was in that moment that something told me to immediately muster my courage and run out of the building. I took one step toward the doors and almost fell. My body had woken from the momentary shock-induced stupor and was telling me that there were a million things wrong with it—and the pain in my left foot was especially insistent. Adrenaline quickly took over, though, and I took one step on my left foot, and then one step on my right.

Over the course of about ten seconds, I made it several feet toward the doors when another explosion rocked the airport forty meters to my right, knocking me slightly off balance as yet another small shock wave ran through my battered body. Luckily, the distance was just enough to protect me from the shrapnel of the second explosion, but the impact of the blast still sent my mind reeling; it felt like the entire building was under attack.

By the grace of God, I stayed on my feet and kept stumbling toward the exit, avoiding felled ceiling panels and shuffling over broken glass and metal. I kept going until I got outside. I knew my body was not in good shape, but I didn't know just how serious my situation actually was. I staggered out of the smoke of the destroyed airport and into the open air. I made it a few more feet and grabbed the handrail opposite the sidewalk. The moment my hands touched the steel, my left leg gave out and I stood gingerly on one foot, trying to get my bearings.

I left Joseph, Fanny, and Richard in the airport. That thought instantly pulled my attention back to the airport terminal. As I glanced toward the smoke billowing out of the wrecked doors and tried to make out which figures could be them, my eyes caught sight of a trail of crimson spots that started in the airport and led right to where I was standing—and when I looked down, I was standing in a pool of my own blood. The fact that I was injured and bleeding copiously from my foot hadn't even registered until now. My mind was in a daze.

As I observed the wound on my left heel for the first time, I realized that I was in trouble. The bomb packed with shrapnel had made quick work of my thin suit pants which now hung in tatters and devastated my left leg. Below that, I saw the source of the blood. The explosion had blown open part of my heel. The skin was gone on the right side, and I could see tissue that should never, ever be visible to the human eye. A very literal stream of blood as though from a sink faucet flowed ceaselessly from the mess of my left heel. I stared at it, trying to come to terms with how profoundly serious my injury was.

I looked down at my torso and noticed that my white shirt was soaked in blood and covered with body tissue. I shuddered as I realized that not all the blood and tissue was my own.

As I stood on the sidewalk trying to collect my thoughts and make sense of what was happening, I felt cemented to the ground. It quickly became apparent that I could no longer move. Though I had walked on my own power away from the blast, here in safety walking was suddenly impossible. That's when a man rushed over to me with a look of bewilderment in his eyes and tried to help.

"You must sit," he commanded.

On one leg and still clinging to the now blood-stained handrail, I let him help me sit in the pool of my own blood.

Now that I could sit, it was as if my body woke up with a vengeance and my pain receptors suddenly remembered what they were supposed to be doing. As they hastened to get back online, my brain was overloaded with signals firing from the tip of my head to a throbbing in my heel. My body hurt all over. I would later come to find that I had taken shrapnel and suffered lacerations to the head, second-degree burns to my face and ear, third-degree burns to my right hand, shrapnel to my right hip and both legs, and shrapnel to my left heel that tore off the skin, ruptured my Achilles tendon, and shattered my heel bone.

The adrenaline that helped me escape the airport before the second blast suddenly wore off, and my head was flooded with thoughts, feelings, and questions at a hundred miles an hour. *Am I still at the airport? I am. Can I hear anything? Only through my left ear. Who did this? Are there more bombs? I can't see my companions through the smoke. Is Elder Empey alive? How bad am I hurt? Wow, that's a lot of blood coming out—I need to stop it.*

The man who was with me interrupted my thoughts. "Do you know where you are?"

"Yes. How bad am I hurt?" I responded, trying hard to sound calm.

"You are very bad, but okay," he said. "We need to stop the bleeding on your foot. Something inside the airport just exploded."

I was well aware.

Just then, a new wave of thoughts flooded into my head, but this time instead of panic, a strange calm came over me. Where just before I was in a mental frenzy, searching and grasping for a dose of reality in a world that no longer seemed to offer any semblance of sanity, I was surprisingly finding myself at peace. Lying there on the frigid sidewalk, the pain was no longer overwhelming. I could see clearly again. I watched as more people stumbled out of the airport, many holding their faces or other body parts, their clothing covered in blood. I was elated when I noticed that one of the individuals streaming out of the building was Sister Clain; she obviously looked injured, but she was walking out with a woman who had suffered burns in the blast.

Seeing her safe and alive brought me relief. She quickly moved past me, not noticing that I was there, and the two disappeared from my view as I looked back toward the terminal. I was looking for Elder Empey, but the sheer number of injured people running back and forth and pouring out of the airport made it impossible to see if he was among them.

As people continued to run away down the sidewalk, screaming in pain and fear, I saw a young Muslim woman in a peach shirt and high heels walking toward the blast instead of away. She was walking toward me. She had noticed me unable to move on the ground and came over to crouch beside me. Her name was Isabel.

"Hey, hey, you're okay," she said as I looked at her with unease. "You're hurt. How can I help you?"

Isabel became visibly emotional when she saw my injuries. Tears swam just at the edges of her eyelids. Though distraught, the look on her face was one of peace. She had the look of an angel, displaying a quiet calm in the storm that made me feel that somehow everything would be okay.

Her presence brought me an added measure of peace. It was at this moment that my preparation as an Eagle Scout finally came full circle and I remembered the basic first aid training that I had learned so many years ago, though I thought, *I never thought I would be using it like this.*

I tried to create a coherent sentence but that proved more difficult than I had expected. I managed to stutter out between wracking coughs, "My body . . . my body might be in shock. I need you to hold . . . hold my hand. My body might start seizing up. I don't want to go into more shock." She took my hand and looked me up and down.

"You'll be okay," she said with the best smile she could put on.

Isabel became a symbol to me—a reminder that even in the most desperate of circumstances suffered by mankind, there are those who possess an unusual allotment of Christ-like qualities of courage and compassion, without which some would surely come to question the very nature of their relationship to the Divine. The faces of most people at the airport were filled with shock and disbelief. Even more were screwed up in absolute panic. In this storm of dark emotions that felt thick in the air, Isabel gave off a much-needed calm.

She sat there with me for a few more minutes, and then Elder Empey came out of the airport, badly injured but alive. He noticed me and came over with a hollow look in his eyes—likely the same look I'd had since exiting the airport.

"Are you okay?" he asked, holding his burnt hands out in front of him.

"Yes, I'm fine. I just saw Sister Clain walk out. She's alive too, but she was hurt pretty bad."

He came over and stood above me for a moment. Isabel looked him up and down as she had me. She continued holding my hand but spoke up to him, "You're hurt just like your friend. Can you move your hands?"

Elder Empey looked down at his hands, but didn't say anything. I could see that his legs had also been peppered with shrapnel, and the skin was hanging in strips off of his face from the burns to his head. Seeing my friend injured really brought home the enormity of the attack to me. We looked at each other, bleeding and broken, and tried to make sense of how our lives had just changed. Even while I looked at the face of my injured companion and I faced momentary shock at the ordeal we had just experienced, I still felt that strange inner peace that directly contradicted the outer turmoil. I was grateful for the stillness.

Empey sat down behind me on the sidewalk in between me and an African man with injured eyes while another good Samaritan attempted to keep him calm. The seconds since the blast stretched on and with each passing moment, other injured individuals laid down around me on the sidewalk. The initial screaming had tempered and transformed into plaintive moans of pain. I wasn't sure which was worse.

Despite the comfort I felt, my heart ached for the people around me. Just eight feet in front of me was a scene that would be forever burned into my memory: there was a woman on her knees, hovering over the body of another woman who'd been blown open from the back of her knees to the middle of her torso. It would be only minutes before she bled out. The woman on her knees locked eyes with me, and I saw the disbelief on her face. In that moment, I could feel the helplessness written on her heart.

I wanted to reach across the cracked concrete and share the peace I felt with her. I wanted desperately to tell her that it was okay—that there wasn't anything she could do to save her friend—that the figure over which she knelt would soon be in a better place. I wanted to let her know that she was loved. But it was impossible to speak the words. And even if I could, my words would never reach her over the din. So, I gently smiled at her and did the only thing I could—pray.

Eventually, the man who had initially examined me came back with a suitcase and asked me to elevate my leg. The bleeding had slowed and my body was shaking less than before.

The man asked for Elder Empey's belt, and Elder Empey gave it to him. Using the belt, he began to tie a tourniquet on my left leg. I realized what he was doing, and stopped him.

"No, no, I don't want a tourniquet," I said in messy French, but he protested, warning of what might happen if he didn't place one on my leg. "Kid, you need this. Your leg needs to be in a tourniquet. You're bleeding very badly."

But I was resolute, telling him through my pain that I wouldn't be dying and that I simply didn't need a tourniquet. I knew what would happen if that tourniquet were tied. It may save my life, but I would almost certainly lose my leg. The tight knot of the tourniquet would stop the blood flowing out of my body, yes. But my leg would cease to get oxygenated blood, and the tissues would start to die. To save my life, I would have to lose my leg. I felt something stirring in me. A confidence in my state that I had not had since exiting the airport. I looked down at my hand—it was black and a very angry red. My leg was leaking what seemed to be all the blood in my body. I could feel the chill on my head from wind cooling the blood coming from a wound I could not see. And yet, I felt that I would survive and I knew that my faith could heal me. In that moment, it was as if something was asking me if I truly believed in God's power to heal. I made up my mind.

I looked him square in the eye and said, "I'm not going to die today, and I want to keep my leg."

He threw the belt on the ground, frustrated, and before walking away to help others, he protested one last time: "Why won't you let me tie it? You are losing too much blood! You will die if I don't do this!" Despite the pain in that moment, I was convinced I would be okay, so I once again declined.

Through it all, Isabel was still holding my hand. I turned my attention back to Elder Empey behind me.

"Elder Empey, do you want a blessing?" I said.

"You're worse than I am. You need the blessing." I nodded and he put both of his burnt hands on my head. In the name of Jesus Christ, he blessed me that I would survive. I don't remember exactly what he said other than that he promised I would "return to life as a normal boy."

As he lifted his hands from my head, the words of a great man, Jeffrey R. Holland, which I had heard in a video the night before, came to my mind: "[God] will keep every promise made to you."[9]

Until that point, I had been praying nonstop in my head for everyone that was there. I started thinking about the people who were responsible for the horrific attack. In that moment, a surprising and profound sense of peace and understanding filled my thoughts. In the absence of anger, humbling clarity filled my emotions. The next prayer in my head was this: *Father, forgive those who have committed this awful deed. Thy justice is right, but give forgiveness unto them according to Thy will. In Jesus's name, amen.*

A powerful peace filled my heart as I offered that prayer, a feeling I believe was an acknowledgment from God that He heard my pleas—that He knew how I felt. Of course, I knew that the Lord understood the pain and suffering that had resulted from the two bombs that had already detonated

Mason on his mission in eastern France.

*Mason with Rep. Jason Chaffetz
and Utah governor Gary Herbert.*

Mason on a bridge next to Notre Dame in Paris.

Mason in Washington, D.C., working as an aide to Rep. Jason Chaffetz.

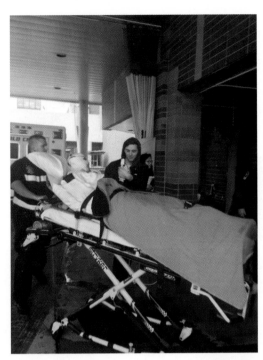

Mason arriving at the University of Utah Hospital.

Preparing to board the air ambulance at an airport in Charleroi.

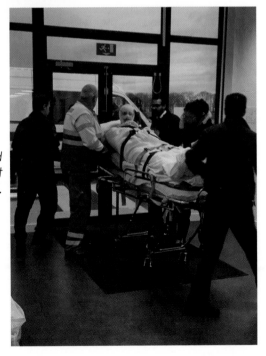

Mason, as a Naval Academy Midshipman, with his siblings.

Mason and his dad on induction day at the Naval Academy.

The Wells family. From left to right (top row): Chad, Mason, Porter, Colby (bottom row): Kymberly, Tayla, and Mia.

(and the third that would detonate shortly thereafter halfway across town at the Schumann metro stop), but the peaceful reaction was a helpful reminder of His presence.

Despite what had happened to me, my mind felt open as I lay on the ground with such grave wounds; I knew that God loved every person who was on that sidewalk. Somehow, with that peace that was infused into my very being, my fear in that moment had entirely dissipated. I knew deep in my gut that I would live and that God would take care of me.

The voice of Elder Empey came from behind me, shaking me from my thoughts: "Mason, I'm going to find Elder Norby." He got up and walked back into the terminal. Five minutes later, he came back.

"He's alive, but he's hurt pretty bad," he told me. "There are people helping him right now." At that point, it hurt too much for him to stand, so he sat on the other side of the suitcase that my leg was propped up on. Through it all, Isabel was still there, holding my hand and talking to keep me awake.

Twenty minutes had passed since the initial blast and the first emergency vehicles were already there. EMTs ran down the sidewalk, passing out every medical supply that they had but unable to focus on any one person due to the sheer volume of the injured.

This was a scene I had grown much too accustomed to as I observed terror attacks during the previous four years. Even the responders were panicked as they moved from one body to the next, assessing injuries without the ability or resources to offer substantial help. As they ran past, I looked at Elder Empey.

"Elder Empey, I think our mission is over," I said.

He looked at me with disbelief but didn't respond.

Yeah, we're definitely going home, I thought.

The EMTs who passed by had placed a large ball of gauze on my burnt hand, but hadn't stopped to do more than that. I had the impression to take the gauze off of my hand.

"Elder Empey," I said, "take this gauze and shove it into the hole in my heel." I gave him the gauze, and he did the best he could to fit it to the wound. After forty-five minutes out on that sidewalk, it was almost my turn for an ambulance.

And after another fifteen minutes passed, I was next in line for medical care. I was grateful to finally escape that freezing sidewalk. A stretcher was pulled up, and six people lifted me in unison, shuttling me down the sidewalk and away from the decimated airport entrance. As they maneuvered me farther away, I caught a more horrific view of the worst of the carnage. I could see debris, blood, smoke—and grieving people. It was much more organized than before, but the panic was almost tangible.

I was transported to the airport fire station before being taken to the hospital. The station was not even fifty yards from where the two bombs had gone off. When we arrived, the building's tall doors had been pulled up, and the three fire engines that would normally occupy the garage were out on the road. They moved me into the building, where some fifty or so wounded were already being attended to. I had been in there for ten minutes, when, once again, all hell broke loose.

As I lay on a stretcher surrounded by other injured individuals and first responders, the moans and screams of the afflicted were interrupted by gunfire. Instantly, chaos and panic again ensued as people just down the road came running toward us and then bolted right past.

The injured—myself included—instantly realized that the danger wasn't over, so we also tried to flee, though many of us simply couldn't due to our injuries. A massive crowd of people ran in front of me with their heads down, ducking for fear of being struck by a bullet. Those running quickly realized that the fire station garage where I was offered shelter from the line of sight of the gunman.

People frantically broke off from the sidewalk and ran through the garage, rushing past cots of injured survivors. The EMTs attending to us followed suit. Shouts of "There's someone with a gun!" and "A man with a Kalashnikov is shooting people!" came as people rushed past my cot. Some of the injured persons were attempting to crawl out the back of the garage.

I knew I wouldn't be able to get that far. The man next to me that had crawled away had left his blanket and so, hoping that I could pass as a pile of blankets, I pulled the sheet over me and laid as motionless as I could. All I could do in that terrifying moment was cover myself with a blanket and pray that any additional terrorists or shooters wouldn't make it to where I was.

I heard more gunshots—and then the panic stopped. The medics, who had fled with in the initial wave of panicked folks, trickled back in to care for us. By the grace of God, the shooter had been stopped, and I was safe.

I received some minimal treatment at the fire station before the ambulance took me to the hospital. There was one responder in the back with me and I asked him if he spoke English.

"I do," he said, "but not very good." In that moment, that was good enough for me.

"How long does it take to get to the hospital?"

He responded, "It takes about uh . . . twenty minutes. It might be a little bumpy."

I tried to get my mind off the pain and continued, "Is this your first run?"

"You are my second," he responded. "The first was much worse, but even though you are serious, I think you will definitely live."

I said, "I hope so," and tried to let out a little chuckle that ended up turning into a painful groan. As we traveled toward the hospital, the pain was getting much worse. I had begun to occasionally grunt as sharp pains would hit me and then quickly abate. For several minutes, I gripped tightly to the cot I was laying on.

In the three and a half hours since the first explosion, I had been praying nonstop. But in that moment, for the first time, I began to pray for myself. I closed my eyes and attempted to control my shaking body. Everything that happened next is as clear in my memory now as it was at the time.

I began my prayer, *Father, thank you for saving my life. However, I am injured and I hurt very badly. Please help me to deal with the pain and ease it for me.* I never finished the prayer, as an incredible peace once again came over me. My body stopped shaking, and I felt God speaking to me: "Mason Scott Wells, you will keep your hand and your foot, and I will confirm this unto you by my Holy Spirit." In an instant, my pain disappeared completely.

Truth be told, the peace that overcame me took me off guard, and for the first time that day, I quietly began to sob.

I remember thinking that the medic must have thought I was a wreck, but the events of the day had finally taken their toll.

The absence of pain and the peace that accompanied that promise stayed with me until I arrived at the hospital. Once there, doctors administered painkillers, and I began my long journey to recovery.

The irony is that March 22, a day filled with so much pain, horror, and uncertainty, ended up being one of the most peaceful days of my life—a fact that I can only attribute to God. Despite pain and horror, I felt His presence telling me that it would all be okay and that I would survive to see another day.

In the end, I will never forget what God did for me that day in the back of that ambulance. There were certainly other miracles from my time in Belgium that reassured and reminded me that God cares for me, but the peace from that prayer proved to me that He has a plan for each of us.

Hope is what has made my recovery possible; the act of attempting with the best of our abilities—and amid uncertainty—to recover shows deep faith. The choice to let go of anger and hate is an act of faith. Hope has carried me through the painful hours of rehabilitation, the despair of slow recovery, and the work to achieve hard goals that I've set out to attain. The incredible thing about hope is that it not only continues to save me, but it has the power to rescue every person willing to embrace it. Hope drives fear from our hearts—it replaces pessimism with optimism and frustration with peace. Hoping is an action that results from choice.

It was hope—and prayer—that made all the difference. I still remember praying ceaselessly from the time the bombs went off throughout my time in the hospital, even as I went in for an MRI and was prepped for surgery. Then, everything went dark.

CHAPTER 7 |
Recovery |

*A journey of a thousand miles
begins with a single step.*

—Lao Tzu[10]

Coming out of surgery felt like waking up in someone else's body. The pulsing pain hit me before I even opened my eyes. Even in my half-conscious state, I could feel piercing spots of cold all over my body. My hand felt immobilized. The minute I even thought about moving it the realization hit me: I could barely feel it. My head was throbbing—the supposedly tiny holes from the stitches on my temple felt as though they were the size of potholes.

The pain in my lower body was even worse. My legs burned and the recently closed wounds from metal pieces of shrapnel felt like tiny red-hot coals were sitting on my skin.

Everything was throbbing painfully. My body simultaneously felt weightless yet intensely sore and heavy. Those, of course, were merely the physical effects.

When I finally came to, I had no idea where I was. What I did know was that I had never felt more uncomfortable. My eyelids felt strangely heavy and my skin felt uncomfortably tight. I struggled to open my eyes, and as they fluttered open, I could see that I was in a big white room with peach curtains around my cot. After a second, I could hear the muffled sounds of people bustling around beyond the curtains. The sudden influx of sound from my damaged right ear was incredibly disorienting. The feedback seemed to suddenly blast through both sides of my head, making me woozy. My senses were so overwhelmed that I couldn't help but drift back to blissful sleep.

When I woke up again, I was a bit more aware of the fact that I was in a hospital. The voices of figures that I could vaguely make out through my burnt eyelids and bandages woke me up from what seemed like a never-ending sleep. My head was still swirling, and I was unbelievably uncomfortable. I tried to realign my body on the bed—an act that proved to be a major mistake. Pain shot down my leg and I let out a brief groan.

"Easy," a voice said. One of the figures resembling little more than a silhouette had put its hand on my left shoulder.

Doing the best I could to wake myself up from a tempting sleep, I opened my eyes again, which was truly a daunting task. Considering everything I had been through, it literally hurt to stay awake. But as I gazed around the room, I realized that there were five people around me. One was obviously a doctor, the others, I presumed, were nurses. The doctor spoke first.

"Mr. Wells, do you know where you are?" he asked. I tried to focus on what he was saying, but my eyes were at half-mast. Somehow, though, I mustered a response.

"I'm at the hospital?" I asked, though I internally knew the answer.

"Yes," he said. "You were very badly injured by a bomb."

The doctor's proclamation triggered my memory, and the traumatic events that unfolded just hours earlier came flooding back to my mind. *My hand, my foot—do I still have them?* I frantically thought. My eyes shot open as I braced myself to be an amputee.

I quickly glanced down at my right hand and noticed that my entire arm from the elbow down was covered in bandages and gauze. On the outside, I could tell that the bandages formed to make five fingers at the end of my arm.

It's still there, I thought, letting out an audible sigh of relief before continuing in my quest to assess the rest of my body.

Now for my leg. I looked down the cot to see what appeared to be my left foot with metal rods sticking out from every which way. My stomach seemed to climb into my chest, as I mentally forced it back down.

It's still there.

The doctor, noticing my brief investigation, started to explain the extent of my injuries. "You had bad burns on your hand and some serious wounds on your foot, but we were able to keep them through surgery," he reassured me.

My body deflated. I was of course grateful to have all my appendages, but I was also acutely aware of the fact that I likely looked horrible. The gauze on my face, I imagined, only made it worse.

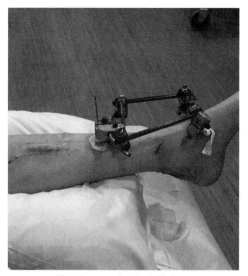

Fixator rods stabilizing
Mason's left ankle, two
weeks after the bombing.

As my initial panic turned to fear and concern over my appearance in the moment, the doctor started speaking again. Still, I couldn't fully focus on what he was saying. Something about the hospital I was at, something about whether I had family, something about the languages I spoke, something about who I was with when the bomb detonated. That last part sparked a memory. *My friends!*

"I had three friends at the airport. Do you know where they are?" I mustered.

The doctor hesitated. "No, but why don't you give me their names and I'll see what I can do. Are your parents from the United States?"

"Yes," I replied. It felt incredibly surreal to be talking so calmly when I was so far from okay. To be talking at all when I had nearly been blown up less than twenty-four hours ago was unreal to me. Had it really only been a few hours?

"Why don't you give me their emails," he said, "and I'll try to find a phone that you can talk to them on." The doctor walked out of the room, and two of the nurses stayed behind, looking at me with kind and occasional glances.

The doctor's silhouette became blurry as he went down the corridor, moving away from my hospital bed as I could feel myself slipping into unconsciousness yet again.

A few minutes later—eight hours after the initial explosion—my parents finally received an email explaining the extent of my injuries.

Later, the doctor once again woke me up. I felt intensely groggy as though I had been asleep for ages, but I knew it had likely only been an hour or two. It took me a minute to gather my thoughts and to remember where I was, as I once again struggled to open my eyes before noticing that the doctor was sitting nearby with a phone in his hand.

I was suddenly more perceptive than I had been just hours earlier, recognizing that the doctor, who was smiling, appeared to be a rather happy guy. We talked again for a few minutes.

"Mr. Wells, I've been emailing back and forth with your parents. They know where you are, and they know how we have treated you. I told them that this will be a long recovery. If you're ready to talk to them, they said they can talk to you right now."

Internally, I was ecstatic. It had been months since I had heard my parents' voices. As missionaries, communication with our families was limited to once a week and only by email. The purpose was to help us focus on the task at hand, while steering us clear of homesickness.

The last time I had spoken with my parents I was serving in a small city called Calais on the northern coast of France. I hadn't yet heard their voices in the year 2016, and it was almost April at the time of the attack. In that instant, I became worried over how my mother was faring with all the information the doctor had given her.

As I sat there listening to the doctor speak, my thoughts drifted to the conversation I had had with my mother the day before over email. She had been giving me news about the family, as always, and had been asking about our work in Brussels:

> MOM: How is Elder Empey? You guys still get along good? When is he done with his mission?
>
> ME: Super good! He finishes in 3 months, 1 transfer before me.
>
> MOM: Any feelings re transfers?
>
> ME: Hoping to stay together. We think we will :)
>
> MOM: Sounds like you guys are the dream team! Checking mail everyday for scholarships from the U. Did you see pics of all the AP credit they accepted?!
>
> ME: Yeah that was great! Have I gotten any scholarships yet?
>
> MOM: Not yet. You got into honors college at Utah State too. Do you realize that there are suburbs in Brussels known for terrorists bases? Do you know bad areas to stay out of?
> The terrorist was found in Molenbeek? Known for housing terrorists. Do you go near there? Just say NO.
>
> ME: No, I don't go in terrorist areas.

As I sat in my hospital bed, that last email exchange—and particularly the last line—played over and over again in my head. I wasn't lying at the time, but somehow, despite not going into the areas my mom perceived as being terror-ridden, I still ended up in a "terrorist area." I took the phone from the doctor as these thoughts started to recede and dialed my dad's number. After one ring, a warm, familiar voice floated from the receiver.

"Hello! Mason, are you there?" my mom said, her voice a striking amalgam of fear, worry, and excitement.

"I'm here," I replied.

My first thirty-six hours in the Aalst hospital were hazy. As the hours and days progressed, my pain grew more and more intense, which meant more and more medication. My body was over the initial shock, and I was forced to deal with the long-term damage. I was moved into a room on the ICU floor that was much quieter than the room where I was initially placed. Throughout that time, there was a steady stream of nurses flowing into my room, changing my many bandages, feeling my face, putting gels on my skin, and just generally poking at my body. So much of it was a blur.

At the end of my first full day at the hospital, I was told that I was going to be moved to a hospital in Ghent, Belgium, due to the nature and extent of my injuries. The Aalst hospital was just outside of Brussels, and the nurses spoke both English and French; I wouldn't be afforded that luxury in Ghent, a city up north where almost everyone spoke Dutch. I wasn't very enthusiastic about the two-hour ambulance ride to the hospital, to say the least, but despite my dread, I was thankful to be able to get good burn care inside a country where I was a foreigner. That was humbling in itself. I was due for a lot more humbling, as my time in the hospital in Ghent included some of the best and worst moments in my recovery.

I remember being unloaded from the ambulance in Ghent and wheeled into the hospital. My first encounter with this new hospital wasn't much different from what I experienced at the Aalst hospital; doctors prodded and probed my body, taking notes and reviewing the comments that the previous doctors sent along with me. They inspected my bandages and placed me in a new gown. But despite the similarities, there was a key—and really quite terrifying—difference: I couldn't understand a word that the doctors and nurses were saying. I knew they weren't keeping things from me, but it felt incredibly helpless to lie there, listening to doctors talk about my wounds and be unable to understand. I tried to glean information from their facial expressions, but that didn't work very well. I settled with not knowing.

The hospital room I was in was well kept and clean, but dark. I'll never forget the awful, dark-orange paint that seemed to drain the light out of every wall and hallway. It wasn't only the walls that felt suffocating, though. The lights in each room were weaker than the ones I was used to. They struggled to illuminate various areas within the hospital, a sharp contrast to the bright lights in Aalst. It's hard to explain how that dingy hospital made me feel. In Aalst, the bright lights made things undeniably cheerier and more hopeful. But like with many good things, I didn't know what I had until it was gone. A seemingly interminable hospital stay seemed that much longer in the dark.

A doctor emerged from the shadows, startling me out of my thoughts. "Hello Mason, I am Dr. Monstrey. I'm going to be helping you while you recover from your injuries."

So, someone does speak English. I breathed a sigh of relief.

He continued, "We've been reviewing your injuries since before you arrived and we're going to . . . uh, put some skin on there."

"Put some skin on it?" I repeated, not quite sure which part of my torn and tattered body he was referring to—or what skin he intended to use, for that matter. My curiosity didn't last long, though.

"Yes, from a uh—ya know, someone that is not alive anymore."

"A cadaver?" I asked.

"Exactly! You have bad burns, but do not worry, we are one of the best hospitals in Europe for these sorts of things. Do you plan on returning to the United States? We can treat you here very well, but the decision is up to you."

I didn't want to seem rude, but I said: "I want to head home as soon as I can, but I trust you here."

"Alrighty," Dr. Monstrey said. "Let's continue."

After that, I was placed in a room by myself with a television and a window with blinds that made it impossible to see out to what was on the other side. I didn't spend much time complaining about my surroundings. Despite the intense pain, I was becoming more grateful for the fact that I had my life—and I chose to reflect on that. In fact, I was relatively peaceful despite my beaten condition. My body was in critical condition, but for the most part my mind was returning to normal.

After my conversation with Dr. Monstrey, the nurses left after a few minutes to prep the machinery I would need for my stay. For the first time in a long time, I was awake and alone. I had spent the last day and a half waking up for bandage changes or when they needed to poke, prod, or work on me; other times, I was asleep or things were simply too foggy for me to focus on my whereabouts. My mind had been a blur of shock and amnesia. But suddenly, in that moment, I was entirely coherent. I sat there motionless for what felt like eons. The only sound I heard was the steady *beep, beep, beep* of my heart rate monitor next to my bed, a sound that was perfectly in sync with the pulse I could feel thumping up and down inside my chest. Aside from my monitors, it was completely silent inside of my room. And that's the first time I truly started to process what had happened to me.

Did this really happen? I had come to terms—in part—with what had happened to me and so many others less than two days earlier. I had seen horrible things. You don't just forget something like that. But when I dreamt and saw the wounded, or heard the screams of those that were embracing death, I chose not to be afraid. I had already forgiven. And rather than remember the terrorists' hatred, I chose to dwell on the acts of heroism I witnessed and their effects. I chose to remember Isabel and the people that had stopped to help me. I chose to remember love.

But as I said, you don't just forget something like that. And though I chose to see the positive, that proved difficult as the horrific scenes played over and over in my mind. Once my mind was allowed to be still, it took me back to the panic—the terror. *I can't be afraid of those memories,* I told myself. *That's no way to live.* As flashbacks shot through my mind amid the room's calm aura, I realized that I had two diametrically opposed options for how I could process those horrible memories. I could see myself either as a victim or as a survivor.

In those moments of vulnerability, it would have been so easy to victimize myself, to ask "Why me?" but I knew that God had stretched forth His hand and saved me. And if an all-powerful God had been willing to step in when I needed Him most, then I had no business feeling sorry for myself. In fact, all of us hold the internal power to soldier on without cocooning ourselves in misery and woe; it doesn't take being engulfed in an explosive fireball to realize our power to overcome.

For me, it was my faith that guided me to that place. As soon as I *chose* to be a force for positive action rather than a man who merely marinated in a pit of despair over the unfair things that had happened to me, my life was transformed.

As I contemplated all of this, the resounding silence was pierced by the return of my nurses who had come back with some medical equipment and food. I gratefully started devouring the piece of wheat bread they had brought me. This was an ordeal, since I had to eat with my uninjured left hand. I'm no southpaw so eating was a struggle, to say the least.

Dr. Monstrey came in a few minutes later. "Mason, it's time for us to change your bandages." My doctors and nurses then began the first of many painful bandage changes that I would experience in Ghent, as I reluctantly but gratefully embraced my new normal.

―――

My parents arrived three days after the attack. I'll never forget the first moment that I saw them enter my hospital room. They looked absolutely exhausted, and they had to wear protective gowns, but they were overwhelmingly happy to finally see me. I was just as thrilled to see them.

Things felt a little easier once they got there. They tracked down English speakers at the hospital, and as a result, I soon had a much better idea of where I was and what was going on with my medical care.

Those days in Ghent provided plenty of opportunities to just think, be still, and ponder. There wasn't much else to do, honestly. As a missionary, I didn't watch TV or listen to the radio. I didn't have a phone either, so I was prepared

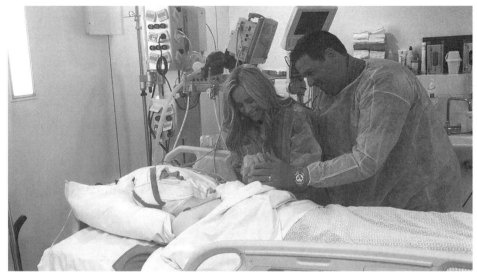

*Mason's parents meeting him at the hospital in Ghent,
three days after the bombing.*

for my time in the hospital. While there, I spent the greater part of each day just thinking—pondering life's mysteries, analyzing my mission, and reflecting on the lives of other people who were hurt or killed in the blasts.

I also spent a lot of time praying. It's incredible how sincere and unrestrained prayer lifted my spirits during those hard days. Many of the thoughtful invocations I offered from that hospital bed were answered with immediate comfort.

I remained resolute that I was unwilling to submit my life to the people who had committed this horrific crime. I knew that if the day ever came in the next life that I was facing the terrorist who so gravely injured me face to face, I would be able to tell him that I had forgiven him for what he did to me. I forgave, but I didn't forget. And I did feel angry at times. But I knew that if I could overcome the natural anger that resulted from the attack, I could overcome any of the difficulties and roadblocks that would impact me throughout my recovery. That reassurance carried me through painful and seemingly endless surgeries and procedures.

One of those incredibly painful operations occurred five days after the bombing. I remember it quite vividly, as it was, hands down, the most painful experience of my life. That morning, Dr. Monstrey came into my hospital room with a few of his nurses.

"Mason, how are you this morning?" he asked. "Feeling better?"

"As good as ever," I let out. *Just another day in paradise*, I thought with an internal eye roll. Then, Dr. Monstrey delivered the not-so-pleasant news.

"We're going to put a nerve block in your armpit this morning—we have an operation to do later today, and your arm must be asleep if we're going to do it."

Great, sounds like more fun, I thought. I was annoyed and irritated with all the procedures, but I tried not to let that show. "What are you doing on this one?" I asked.

"Ah, well if you really want to know, we're going to remove the dead tissue that is on your right hand. We treated your hand yesterday with the fluid I was telling you about, and now we need to get rid of the extra stuff," Dr. Monstrey said.

Not to get too graphic, but the fluid the doctor was referring to was an extraction agent that separated the dying tissue on my hand from the healthy, living tissue. It was experimental. I was asleep when they performed the initial procedure, but I would be awake for the extraction.

"Well, let's get at it," I said, not quite sure how enthusiastic I really was to face the unexpected. The nurses prepared the nerve block, and soon enough they were pressing

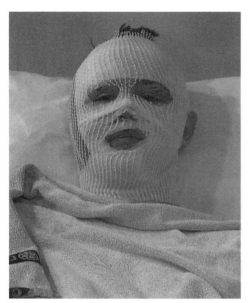

Mason at the hospital being treated for third-degree burns.

the largest needle I had ever seen in my life into my skin.

As the hours pressed on, though, the nerve block wasn't working. It was supposed to knock out my arm so I couldn't feel anything during the procedure, but I still had full feeling in my right arm hours later. The nurses had come in several times to try and fix it, but to no avail. Despite taking it out, attempting to put a new one in, and poking around my arm, there was no use. The clock was ticking, and the extraction would soon be happening

Dr. Monstrey came in after the third catheter placement. "Well," he began, "we have to do this procedure today. Did the last nerve block do anything? Can you feel your arm?" he asked with a hopeful look on his face.

"It's not working at all," I said.

His eyebrows wrinkled. He was obviously frustrated, and he didn't try to hide it from me. He brought his hand to his chin and looked at the bed pensively for a few seconds, clearly struggling to think of alternatives. He then turned and ushered over one of the nurses; they exchanged words that I didn't understand before he went back to thinking a bit more, resuming his signature chin stroking.

"Well," he started, "you took pain meds a few hours ago, so we can't give you anything to swallow or put anything in your IV. At the same time, if we don't take off that skin now, we could risk damaging your hand and delaying your healing."

I could tell the gears were turning; he had a decision to make. "Can you do this without a nerve block?" he asked.

I don't know what "this" is, I thought. From the look on his face though, I could tell it would be a rough operation. *I've been through a lot of pain already, so how bad could this be?* I weighed the possibilities in my head. Ultimately, damaging my hand any further wasn't an option.

I looked at Dr. Monstrey with cautious determination and proclaimed, "Let's do it."

The next half hour was the most painful thirty minutes of my life. I clenched my teeth and writhed in pain as the doctor scraped flesh off the exposed third layer of skin on my right hand—with no painkillers. Within the first minute of the procedure, the doctors could tell that I was having a rough time. One of the men who was just spectating, a doctor with thin, black-rimmed glasses, came over to me and offered to hold my left hand. I immediately took him up on the offer.

"You will be all right," the doctor said. "This will be over. Don't look over there, just look at me. Let's talk."

Then, he began to ask questions to distract me. "What was a nineteen-year-old doing in Brussels?" he asked.

Amid the horrific pain, I decided to focus on the doctor and began to tell him about my life. I told him about life as a missionary and explained our message of God, and ironically, he listened more attentively than many of the people I had taught during my mission. He was an atheist, but I was a patient, so he quietly entertained my proclamations in between my occasional screams. For thirty minutes we talked about God, the purpose of family, where we came from, and where we were heading in life.

Sharing my beliefs with him took away some of the pressure from the pain and anguish I was experiencing. At one point, I prayed that I would have the energy and stamina to finish sharing my faith with him. At that very moment, a feeling of comfort overtook me; we were able to finish our discussion.

When the operation was finally over, the doctors had cleared my room, but I truly believe that I could feel the presence of angels from a world beyond the gaze of my mortal eyes. Once again, God was comforting me when I had done my best to reach out to Him in my time of need.

In the days after the operation, my time in Ghent went much more smoothly. Sure, there were more of those painful bandage changes and uncomfortable medical procedures, but I was through the worst of it.

On the morning of March 31, I rode in an ambulance to the airport in Charleroi, ready and more than willing to continue my journey of healing. The FBI was flying me home to Utah—a 14-hour flight that I would take via air ambulance. The intricacies involved in my trip back were breathtaking. There were two drivers on the air ambulance, an air medical technician, my mom, and me. The air ambulance only allowed one of my parents to come with me, so my dad elected to take a commercial flight home to Utah. After a long drive, our ambulance pulled up to the tarmac of an airport in Charleroi.

Due to the events of the previous days, security was heightened and military troops had been deployed across the country. As our ambulance came up to the security checkpoint, five masked men with Kalashnikov-style assault rifles circled our vehicle. They stopped us and began probing the driver as to why we needed access to the airfield. When our driver told them that I was connected to the bombings in Brussels, their suspicion mounted. Belgian authorities were still tracking down terrorists that were part of the attacks, and anybody attempting to leave the country by air raised eyebrows.

We waited for five minutes as several of the men sought to validate the legitimacy of our flight. Ten minutes passed, then fifteen. No one had cleared us yet, and we were starting to get worried about missing our take-off time. My mother, understandably, was scared at the appearance of masked, armed men in the dark hours of the early morning as we were merely trying to get back home. The medical technician in the back with me was also getting frustrated.

"We're at the wrong airport!" she suddenly exclaimed. Sure enough, our drivers had taken us to the wrong location. Here we were without a flight yet seemingly attempting to get onto the tarmac. It must have seemed like suspicious behavior to authorities who were still grappling with the series of coordinated terror attacks that had left the government on full alert. My mom about lost it.

Our drivers were too hesitant to admit their mistake to the masked men, and so my medical technician angrily flew out the back of the ambulance to solve the problem. The soldiers understandably eyed us menacingly as we turned around and headed to the other airport, but there was no further incident. Luckily, we reached the proper location, and I was loaded into the airplane with just minutes to spare.

As we took off and ascended into the clouds, I stared somberly at the ground beneath us, recalling the flood of lifelong memories—both good and traumatizing—that I lived out in Brussels. It was time for a new chapter, indeed.

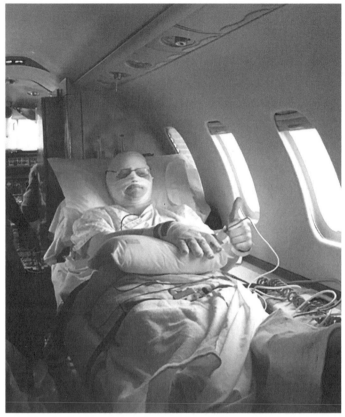

*Mason in the air ambulance
returning to the States.*

CHAPTER 8 |
Back Home |

Hope is being able to see that there is light despite all of the darkness.

—Desmond Tutu[11]

I arrived in Utah in the middle of an intense snowstorm, leaving me unable to see more than a hundred feet in any direction. *Home, sweet home*, I thought, as the plane's wheels finally touched the ground after what felt like a nearly eternal journey back home. A medical transfer was waiting for me when we landed, and I was promptly loaded up and transported to the University of Utah Hospital in Salt Lake City—yet another facility where I would continue my recovery.

It's funny: when you're gone from a familiar place for quite some time and suddenly return, you tend to see things through new lenses, having a newfound appreciation for some of the things that you once took for granted. Case in point: For the first time in years, I noticed road signs and billboards in English as the ambulance rolled down the paved city streets. The cars all looked so much larger and the roads so much wider than I remembered, especially in contrast to the vehicles and streets in France and Belgium.

As I took it all in, I couldn't fully grasp the fact that I was back in the United States—*back home*. It felt strange to see American stores and Western brands on every street corner and to be immersed in the intensely familiar scenes that had formed and shaped my experiences as a youth. But after the flurry of chaotic events that unfolded, that familiar environment offered a welcome solace.

Arriving at the hospital yielded a sweet moment. My seventeen-year-old brother, Colby, was the first to make his way over to me as medical personnel unloaded me from the ambulance; he wouldn't leave my side until the doctors told him that he absolutely had to. When we entered the ICU, it again struck me how bizarre it was that every nurse and resident doctor spoke perfect English, as I had to once again remind myself that I was back stateside. As the paramedics wheeled my bed down the trauma unit, the thirty or so medical personnel all stopped to make way for me. An eerie silence overtook the hospital floor as I felt dozens of eyes turn their attention toward me. Their gazes followed me all the way down the hallway. I was puzzled for a second, until I realized that I probably looked pretty rough with my entire head, foot, and left hand all wrapped up in gauze. My parents confirmed to me later that I did look badly beaten up.

I was quickly moved to the hospital's burn unit to continue my recovery; for the first few weeks, the poking and prodding by doctors, nurses, medical technicians, and CNAs renewed with a vengeance, as each performed a different task to ensure that I would eventually get back to full health. While I was grateful for the ministrations of the staff on my behalf, the circus that took place in my room day in and day out quickly got old. I was sick of the attention and frustrated with the slow healing process. I'd always been really active and self-sufficient, so being waited on wasn't natural for me. And not being able to move around was really starting to grate on me.

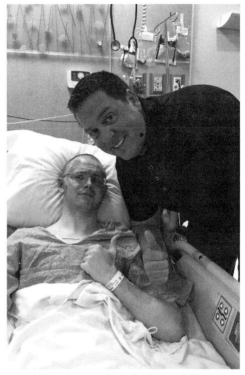

Mason and his father at the University of Utah Hospital in Salt Lake City.

During my first week at the hospital, though, I was delivered a pleasant surprise. I was stunned to see Elder Empey being wheeled into my room. He had flown out of Brussels the day before and was placed in the same burn unit.

"Elder Wells!" he exclaimed as the nurse brought him in. "How are you, man?"

I was so happy to see him I couldn't help but laugh. "Elder Empey! You look great, dude! So, they've got you in a wheelchair too, huh?" Empey was able to come over to my bed and we embraced for the first time in a long while. He had been an incredible companion, and still had his signature cheery smile—that familiar expression that I knew well from our time serving together overseas.

Empey progressed much quicker in his recovery than I did. In fact, he was up and walking around the burn unit floor in no time while I was still confined to a bed and a wheelchair. After a week, the doctors were willing to offer me a walker on two conditions: (1) that I hopped on one foot, and (2) that I was always attended to. The walker was a welcome form of mobility and a breath of fresh air, though it would be another two months before I could walk normally.

Because I was in bed most the time, I received a blood thinner shot once a day to keep everything running smoothly. Dr. Bagley let me know that I could avoid the blood thinner shot if I was willing to hop nine laps around the burn unit every day using my walker. Nine laps was certainly a lot, but I was getting sick of that blood thinner shot. Plus, my competitive spirit kicked in.

So, around two weeks after the terror attack, I began the first of many laps using my walker. I'm sure the entire hospital heard the *screech . . . screech . . . screech* of my walker legs, as I scraped across the burn unit floor, moving as quickly as my worn body would allow. I would hop, catch my breath, hop, catch my breath, and so on until I had made my slow, sweaty way around the unit nine times. It was a start.

I was determined not to let the terror attack that had already stolen so many days from my life slow me down any further, and so I hopped my heart out to try and get my strength back. There were survivors in the burn unit that didn't do their laps or were unable to get out of bed for one reason or another. I knew that I was physically able to get up every day, but that didn't prevent the temptation of staying idle from entering my head.

It takes too much effort, I thought. *It's going to take ages for me to get better, anyway. I can just sleep today.* Every time a doubt or a hesitation entered my head I had to remind myself that I was working toward a greater goal.

If you truly want to get back to where you were, this is what it takes, I would remind myself. My personal desire to attend the Naval Academy was still intact even if my body wasn't, and I was determined to not only recover, but also to get in shape for my military aspirations. *If you want to get in to the Naval Academy, you need to be willing to work harder,* I constantly reminded myself, using it as fuel to improve. My dream is what drove me to get up day after day and keep trying my absolute hardest. That walker was—and still is—a symbol of humility and perseverance for me. Each hop reminded me that God had preserved my life, and that, though I had been laid low, with Him I could come back better and stronger than before. That walker reminded me that I was no more above the reach of adversity than every other human on the planet—and that I needed to be a little better and work a little harder to be the kind of person I wanted to be.

My end goal was to see the Lord's promise fulfilled, to return to life as a normal young man. I knew I couldn't reasonably expect to lie around while that just happened to me. I would have to work and struggle, and at times, the struggle was the only part of the journey I could see. In the end, despite the surgeries, bandage changes, and procedures, I had to remind myself that I was one of the lucky ones; I was alive, my injuries would heal, and that was enough cause to keep living.

After a month, I was fairly comfortable with life on one leg. By that point, doctors had grafted skin onto my damaged right hand and left foot. The graft on my right hand had taken and was progressing, but the graft on my foot had failed. So I was still hopping around the burn unit, pressing on amid a mixture of medical successes and challenges.

Physical therapy was challenging, more mentally than physically, particularly due to the lack of control I suddenly had over my own body. I previously played football and lacrosse and ran track in high school. As a guy who loved sports, being at the mercy of my body rather than controlling my appendages at will was insanely frustrating. Every morning, my physical therapist, Jenny, would come into my room bright and early to wake me up, if my alarm hadn't done so already.

"Wake up!" she would say, bursting through the door at 8 a.m. sharp. I would usually set my alarm for 7:55 to try and be up in time for her arrival, but I was typically too groggy to wake up adequately before she came in. It didn't help that I got horrible sleep most nights because I was so uncomfortable. I would not recommend trying to sleep with dozens of stitches all over your body. Not ideal sleeping conditions, let me tell you.

"Jenny, we don't have to do this," I complained one morning, knowing that I was getting out of the bed regardless of whether I wanted to or not.

"Yes, we do. Otherwise, one day you won't be able to use your hand and do all the crazy things you want to do," she shot back.

I knew she was right. *Well, she sure knows how to motivate me*, I thought. I got out of bed and put on my scrub top. When I initially entered the hospital, they put me in a traditional hospital gown just like everybody else. But as I was particularly motivated to get better and did my laps with the walker every day, the hospital staff got sick of seeing my rear end through the gown as I hopped around, so they upgraded me to hospital scrubs. The scrubs were much more comfortable, so it was a welcome change.

Jenny stayed close as I hopped to my walker and then to the physical therapy room. As always, she had the hand wheel and a bunch of Velcro weights ready for me near a table. Other patients were in the room, doing various exercises and working out the weak parts of their own bodies.

I put my bandaged hands on the hand wheel, and began turning. After fifteen minutes, Jenny strapped Velcro weights to both of my legs, and I proceeded to do flutter kicks, stretches, and abdominal crunches. From there, there was more stretching, an elastic band routine, more weights, and coordination exercises. These sorts of grueling routines filled my mornings, giving me added mental confidence to get through the day.

In the final weeks before I left the hospital, my parents would often wheel me over to the southwest side of the building, where there was a long walkway between two towers that overlooked the entire Salt Lake Valley. I would park my wheelchair, and there, with the wind whipping through my hair, I would gaze out over the city skyline. It was beautiful.

As I stared on in wonder, I would imagine a time when I wasn't in a wheelchair. I would imagine a body that wasn't held back by so many physical limitations. I knew that where I would eventually end up would depend on me and my choices, but as I worked toward that goal, it was sometimes hard not to feel like a prisoner in my own body. As I looked out over that skyline, I committed to being patient. *I'm on God's time right now*, I reminded myself. *Things will work out. He's promised me that.* Reminding myself of God's promise helped allay the frustration I was feeling and motivated me to get back to work and challenge myself to improve.

Seven long weeks after I survived the blast, it was time to go home. I had been through a lot. I had had endured over three hundred stitches and two hundred staples, had braved dozens of incredibly painful bandage changes, and had undergone seven surgeries. My body and my mind were exhausted. But despite the fatigue, I had renewed strength at the thought of finally going home. It had been years since I left for my missionary work, and I was more than ready for the respite.

I'll never forget the day we left the hospital and what it felt like when our car passed through familiar, tree-lined streets and I saw my house for the first time in two years. It was amazing how new the familiarity felt to me, if that makes sense. Still, I was elated to be back home with my family. My dad parked the car in the driveway and then came to help me into my wheelchair. He wheeled me to the edge of the front porch and then stood back to let me hop my way up the stairs. I opened the door and stood in the middle of the entryway, taking it all in. My dad brought my chair up behind me and then left to unpack our stuff from the car. I sat in my wheelchair and looked around at my house. I was finally home. And I was alone.

I could see out the large window in our family room that faced the stunning mountains and valleys surrounding our home. I sat there, thinking about how much I had missed Utah's mountains. And I thought about how close I had come to never seeing them again. And for the first time since my ambulance ride in Belgium, I cried. I couldn't help myself; my heart was a riot of emotion. Joy at being reunited with my family, wonder looking at the beauty of God's creation, awe at how close I came to death, frustration with my weakened body, and gratitude for my life. Experiencing those conflicting feelings all at once overwhelmed me.

It was surreal to think that I had been in the middle of two explosions just two months beforehand, and the memories of that day hit me then, in the safety of my home, a world away from where I had been.

In that moment of intense emotion, I craved peace and comfort. I offered up a prayer of gratitude, and, yet again, as He had done many times in the past after I prayed, God gave me the peace I so desperately needed. It took me a few minutes to gather myself together, and once my heart had calmed, I felt more hopeful. I felt a renewed belief in the promises of the Lord and knew that though the road ahead seemed long, there was a light at the end.

I knew that if I wanted to recover and eventually get into the Naval Academy, I had a lot of work to do. I unlocked my brakes, and rolled my wheelchair into the next phase of recovery.

Time finally seemed to speed up a bit once I was home and sleeping in my own bed. I still had my limitations, but the freedoms were more than worth it. Sure, I still had to take baths since the nurses didn't trust me enough to let me shower on one foot. But things like that were only minor annoyances.

Overall, I was much more comfortable than I had been in the hospital. I still needed a lot of medical attention, unfortunately, so the hospital came to me in the form of home nurses. The biggest health obstacle was my heel.

Initially, I had a wound vacuum placed on my heel to help grow the tissue there while I waited for my next surgery. My hand posed fewer problems. After over three hundred staples, it was finally grafted and had a far simpler set of bandages on it.

I had definitely come a long way since my initial hospitalization in Aalst, but most of my time was still spent lying down and sleeping. I watched quite a few movies, and I finally accepted that I couldn't force my hand and foot to get better immediately. I surrendered to the process.

Over time, functionality returned. It was at home that I was finally able to learn how to write with my right hand again. This was a triumph because since I had been in the hospital, I'd been struggling to write with my left hand. To put it simply: it wouldn't have been a stretch to attribute my handwriting to a struggling kindergartner. I did eventually reach a near-ambidexterity, though that ability was no longer needed once my hand's functionality improved. Still, you celebrate the little victories. It's part of what makes the long road bearable.

As for my progress walking, I took my first step on my left foot a little more than three months after the airport attack. It was a hesitant and cautious step in which I only put about 10 percent of my weight on my foot, holding on to my bed frame in the process.

To be honest, that first step was incredibly discouraging. I could hardly put any weight on it, and I still couldn't walk—I couldn't even limp. The added metal fixator sticking out of my heel made me feel that much more helpless. I was mentally exhausted and by all accounts a physical wreck, lamenting over the fact that, after three months, I couldn't even put one foot in front of the other and balance myself.

I could feel my face getting hotter and hotter. *Why can't my leg just do what I want it to?!* I made three more attempts to put weight on my foot with no more success than the first. I took a second to calm my racing thoughts and tamp down the frustration I was feeling. As I had many times throughout my recovery, I slowly let myself down to my knees and offered a sincere prayer to God. I told Him how angry I was that I couldn't see any improvement. I told Him that I was grateful for my life, but I wondered when it would start back up again. The answer I got was to trust the promises of the Lord. He had promised to return me to health, and He would follow through. I just had to make sure that I would follow through, too. When I opened my eyes, my head was a little clearer.

I'm going to get better—I refuse to give up. Using my bed frame to hoist myself up, I took a few more steps. And I did a little more every day. Slowly, I started to improve. I eventually moved from a wound vacuum on my left foot to a walking boot that was about as thick and tough as Kevlar, or that was how it felt anyway. It was like walking with a cinder block on my foot—but I *could* walk, and that was a victory. With the boot came permission to use the gym—a welcome change from the mundane routine I had been following at home.

My first day at the gym was exhausting. Three and a half months of lying on beds and couches had wreaked some serious havoc on my body and my stamina. When I arrived at the gym to work with a trainer named Mr. Banks, he greeted me with a warm smile and said, "You look a lot better now than you did on TV."

I couldn't help but laugh. "Good to hear," I responded. We talked back and forth and got to know one another before he announced that it was time for me to work out—or at least try to.

After a few moments of silence, a mischievous smile stretched across his face, and Mr. Banks proclaimed, "I know where we're going to start, but you're not going to like it." That smile was suddenly no longer as inviting, and I had a sinking feeling he was right.

We started working out and it quickly became evident that I was significantly weaker than I was before the accident. I had gone from 170 pounds down to 150 pounds over the course of my hospital stay, and my left leg muscles had atrophied quite a bit from the extended bed rest. I tasted the now familiar bitter taste of disappointment as I saw how far I had yet to go.

I'm never going to get in shape in time to get into the Academy, I thought as I struggled to do the leg raises Mr. Banks prescribed. But again, I tried hard to shake off that bit of pessimism and replace it with something to motivate me: *The only way I'll get* anywhere *is by work and dedication*, I reminded myself. But my internal pep talk was interrupted by the sound of Mr. Banks's voice.

"Get those legs higher!"

I grimaced and tried to follow his orders, pushing myself harder. I just kept thinking that the only one who was going to change anything was me, so I lifted my legs yet again. It was the official start of my foray back into athletics and the first step of my journey to get back into shape.

If this were a movie, this is where the workout montage would go. So imagine your favorite upbeat music and fast-forward a couple weeks. I ran for the first time four and a half months after the Brussels blasts. During that time, I'd traded my Kevlar cinder block boot for normal running shoes, and I could walk with only a slight limp. That day, I had just gotten back from the gym and was feeling better than I'd felt in a long time. I was starting to feel like my old self again and something told me deep in my heart and soul that it was time to take my workouts to the next level. So I got out of my car and walked out onto our quiet residential street. It was early, and the sun was just beginning to peek out over the Rocky Mountains. The trees swayed gently in the warm summer breeze, and it felt like the entire world was just barely waking up. I, however, felt ready to once again challenge myself.

I stopped in the middle of the road and locked my eyes on a mailbox that was fifty yards away. In my heart and mind, the decision had already been made: I was about to jog for the first time since before the terror attack. I loosened up, ran in place for a few seconds, and then knelt in starting position.

I could feel the weakness in my left leg, but I felt ready. With a deep breath, I pushed off with my left foot and I just kept on going. I landed push after push until I was in a full sprint. The gravel felt loose underneath my feet, as I consciously tried to land my feet in parts of the street where there was none. In no time at all, I had successfully run fifty yards toward the mailbox on a leg that just four months before had been shattered and needed metal to hold everything together.

I cleared the mailbox and a cheer erupted from my chest. I couldn't help the smile that spread across my face—I had done it. I could finally run. I slowed down and turned back toward the house. My mom was standing in the doorway with a wide smile plastered across her features that matched mine.

"Finally!" she yelled.

"Finally," I responded.

As the days progressed, I could do more and more. I could run farther, work out longer, and walk steadier. I could feel myself getting stronger. I was thrilled to find that my goals were nowhere near as unattainable as I had feared. The future before me was becoming increasingly brighter.

CHAPTER 9
My Navy Calling
Revisited

*What you get by reaching your goals
is not nearly as important as what you
become by reaching them.*

—Zig Ziglar[12]

At the time of my mission service, I had accepted that my goal of attending the Naval Academy would not come to fruition, but my desire to serve in the military was just as strong as ever. My mission changed me, but it didn't change my aspirations. Working through the physical handicaps that the TATP bomb left me with was certainly difficult. Despite the obstacles, I entertained the hope that I could still one day get into the Naval Academy. In fact, I determined that I would reapply in the face of what seemed impossible. I'd beaten the odds once before.

It was easier said than done. Many times, I felt like giving up. *You'll never make it. You came close, but it's not your destiny*, I'd sometimes think. But each time I skeptically reflected and thought of the daunting tasks in front of me, I had to remind myself of where I had been. The person I became on my mission and the person I always grew up being was not gone just because something horrible had happened to me. Sure, things were different; my life had changed over the span of five minutes and I'd fought for months to gain lost ground. But that was just it. Ultimately, I was a fighter. I was still determined to accomplish the things I knew I could.

The tragedy of life, for me, would have been simply giving up on my goals. Broken dreams can be put back together, but purposefully shattering my own desires because I was afraid of disappointment would have irreparably broken me. After recovering from devastating injuries, I wasn't about to let fear rule my actions or paralyze me. I couldn't do that after Boston, certainly not after Brussels, and absolutely not here. So I worked. Six months after the explosions, I was rock climbing again. At seven months, I was no longer limping. At eight months, I was snowboarding and running long distances again. At ten months, *I was accepted into the Naval Academy class of 2021.*

When I was finally accepted, I was speechless. Not because I was shocked, but because there was nothing more to say. I had pulled out all the stops, ran every distance, and completed every task that I needed to do. Many times, I had willingly pushed past laziness and idleness to achieve something that would otherwise have been impossible. Every groan, yell, prayer, late night study, workout, college class, or interview that I could perform was finished, and I was *finally accepted.*

I felt the hand of the Lord. I felt the power of His promises. I had returned to my life, and this was finally what He wanted for me. Being accepted into the Naval Academy was a big weight lifted off of my shoulders. I felt and continue to feel intense pride. When you work toward something you feel is important, never give up. Work as hard as possible to reach your goal. Even if things don't work out the way you want them to, forge on. You might face rejection like I did, but continue down the path.

Receiving the Naval Academy letter of acceptance from former congressman Jason Chaffetz.

My naval ordeal taught me that, often times, God's timing is not our own and we must always seek to follow God's path, knowing full well that He wants what is best for His children. I learned perseverance and determination. I learned to never give up. Overcoming the difficulties of Brussels and coming back stronger than ever has given me incredible insight. I have gone through what was, hopefully, the most difficult, painful, trying thing that will ever happen to me. I got through it with God. I can look back on that in times of trial and know that "I can do all things through Christ which strengtheneth me" (Phillipians 4:13, KJV). This doesn't mean that I am always perfectly patient. It can still be tough, but if we can push past that and rely on

Him, He will guide us down the right path toward what He has set for us.

It makes me smile to think back again at my childhood when I would dress up as an American soldier and pretend to serve my beloved country. It makes me proud to think that I have achieved my childhood dream in spite of unforeseen and nearly fatal roadblocks. Just remember: no matter what your goal, reaching it might not come easy, but nothing I've talked about in this book is all that simple. Recognizing our dreams takes an insane amount of time, focus, perseverance, and dedication. In my own case, the joy is that after all I've been through, I can now put on that blue Navy uniform, look myself in the mirror, smile, and know that this is no longer pretend—that all the blood, sweat, and tears paid off. I made it.

First day of the academic year at the United States Naval Academy.

CHAPTER 10 |
Life Lessons |

We love because he first loved us.

(1 John 4:19, NIV)

About six months after the Brussels bombing, the pieces of my tattered life were beginning to weave back together. I decided to start attending the University of Utah, and on December 7, 2016, I finished my last midterm of my first semester before beginning a leisurely walk back to my dorm. Snow was lightly falling as the sun was struggling to break through the gray storm clouds that blanketed the sky.

As I headed back toward my room, I lifted my eyes to the mountains and saw in the distance a familiar hospital situated on the side of nearby hill—the place where I had spent so much time after arriving back in the US from Belgium. In an instant, I envisioned myself back inside my hospital room, looking out over this same cold, wet valley—but from the opposite side of the mountain range, where I spent grueling hours, days, and weeks recovering from my injuries, both physical and mental. Back then, I could never have imagined the life I was currently living.

Mason, Elder Empey, and Sister Clain displaying their matching compression gloves.

The goodness of God had directed my life—and my recovery—in remarkable fashion. I could never have imagined the happiness and blessings that the Brussels trial would bring. And I certainly could never have anticipated the good that would come rising from the ashes. Don't get me wrong: the experience was terrible and not one I'd wish on my worst enemy, but I learned an incredibly poignant lesson about the reality of God and His love for His children. Seven months after I nearly lost my life in a distant and foreign land, I could now clearly see that God had been with me every step of the way.

As I gazed up toward the hospital where I spent so many days and nights battling my injuries, I stood out in the cold and offered a reflective prayer of gratitude. In the peaceful view of the mountains, I recalled all the incredible things I had witnessed over the past few years. I understood at that moment that one of God's greatest miracles *is us*.

On a broader scale, I've come to learn from my experiences that miracles are very real. That God is real and He is involved in our lives. I'm a living testament to that fact.

It is difficult to explain why a twenty-year-old guy has tasted so much of the bitter fruits of hate. I have tried to reconcile the apparent randomness of these attacks. I've been looking for answers, but they haven't all come at once. There are some things I know and there are things I'm still looking for. I know that God lives, that He saved me, and that He loves all of His children. Why I went through those things—well, I'm still working on that. But my faith in Jesus Christ has led me to ponder on an important verse:

> "For my thoughts are not your thoughts, neither are your ways my ways," declares the Lord.
> "As the heavens are higher than the earth, so are my ways higher than your ways and my thoughts than your thoughts." (Isaiah 55:8–9, NIV)

I feel as though these experiences, though traumatic, have given me a chance to publicly testify about God's love. Despite the attacks, or perhaps because of them, God has blessed me with the ability to feel true empathy for others— even those responsible for these horrific attacks, rather than feeling hatred for them. This alone is a miracle in my eyes. When I would otherwise be inclined to wish malice and revenge on evil men and view the world as a dangerous, dark place, I have been given the gift of peace. It would have been so easy to be angry at God, wondering "Why?" But I chose to rely on the Almighty, and I'm so thankful God has given me the heart to do so. "Why not me?" is a more appropriate question. Bad things can and do happen to all people regardless of belief, race, circumstance, etc. Life happens

Mason and Elder Norby months after the bombing.

and there are events that are out of our control. The only thing we can control is ourselves.

I am grateful that the Lord was with me when I felt alone in that airport. I am grateful beyond measure that He eased my physical pain when I called out to Him in that ambulance and in the hospital. And I am equally grateful that He has been there to speak peace to my emotional pain—that pain that is harder to isolate and treat. Whenever I have sought Him, He has been there. I am thankful that I could learn from King Solomon and ask the Lord for a discerning heart (see 1 Kings 3, NIV). I have been able to put myself in the shoes of others, to feel genuine sorrow for the loss of another, and to be grateful for—rather than resentful of—another's accomplishments. I have seen God in moments of terror and tragedy, and I have seen His hand in times of peace and plenty. I have seen grand interventions on my behalf, and I have seen small, simple things that came together for my good. I do believe that God has a plan for each of us, and that plan does allow freedom of choice. I have seen people use their freedom of choice to harm the greatest number of people possible, and I have seen others use that same freedom of choice to walk toward a bomb site—rather than away—to help a young Christian missionary lying bleeding on a sidewalk.

————————

I want this book to confirm that love isn't just the alternative to hate, but it is also the very thing we need to improve our lives, the lives of those around us, and the world in which we live. All you need is love—love of self, of country, of God, of your fellow man. Love can defeat any evil and triumph over any tragedy. When evil seems pervasive and the light seems dim, love endures. I want to use my story—and the uncommon connection to three horrific attacks—to help restore faith in humanity. Here are the specific lessons that I've taken to heart:

In the end, it all boils down to forgiveness.

As I stood in shock, trying to come to terms with a violent attack on innocents, I had already experienced forgiveness many times. I knew that giving people the chance to move on from their mistakes was the most empowering act of love. And in the end, love is both the motivating force and the end result of active forgiveness. It may be love for those that have harmed us. It may be love for our family—or, as was the case in Brussels—it might be love for a complete stranger who has done immeasurable harm. In every case, forgiveness is about the decision to sacrifice grudges, long-standing anger, and other damaging emotions.

Forgiveness is a difficult concept to live out, as I've learned. But while it is an act of love for others, the decision also protects our hearts: it frees us of the anger, spite, and rage that can spiritually sicken us. Those emotions don't hurt the other person who wronged us so much as they plague our hearts and minds. And given the forgiveness that Christ has offered me, His decision to sacrifice Himself on the cross after praying so fervently in the Garden of Gethsemane, how could I deny others the forgiveness they deserve? Christ forgives all men, and I am certainly not greater than Him.

As hard as it can be to process, I know—and even knew deep down inside right after those bombs detonated—that God still loves the men who committed these heinous acts. My first prayer on the airport sidewalk was for those who were injured. My second was for those that had detonated the bombs—that God would have mercy on them. I do not know to what degree God administers mercy in every situation, but I know that praying for them, with sincerity, and with the true desire to forgive, brought instant relief to my heart, mind, and soul. I didn't let myself consider anger; I wouldn't let myself be brought to bitterness. The feeling of calm that I felt, regardless of the horror surrounding me, is what I believe Christ taught us to seek when He said: "Peace I leave with you, my peace I give unto you: not as the world giveth, give I unto you. Let not your heart be troubled, neither let it be afraid" (John 14:27, KJV).

If given the opportunity, I would have looked the terrorist who injured me in the eyes, shaken his hand, and told him that I have forgiven him for every injury, every bit of pain, every grueling moment of recovery that I was forced to endure after that day. And sometimes forgiving can be hard. But it is a process, like repentance, or healing from a wound. The book *The Shack* by William Paul Young illustrates this very principle. In the book, the portrayal of God says, "You may have to declare your forgiveness a hundred times the first day and the second day, but the third day will be less and each day after, until one day you will realize that you have forgiven completely. And then one day you will pray for his wholeness."[13] No one is beyond our Savior's love. No one.

Positivity makes all the difference.

In addition to embracing forgiveness, I had to choose to have a positive outlook. Both immediately following the attack and in the subsequent months, I had to make some very concrete mental choices. Mainly, I had to choose to be optimistic, believing in the immediate wake of the attack that I would survive and would come out as a whole person with everything the way it was before. That hope is what gave me comfort during the hard times. But I can't take credit for the strength to muster such thoughts—God supplied all the necessary comfort. In the end, I've learned that decisions truly do determine our destiny,[14] and that making the right ones—particularly when it comes to our reactions—can be the difference between peace and misery.

There's a famous phrase that perfectly summarizes this paradigm: "Life is 10 percent what happens to you and 90 percent how you react to it." When you pause and think about it, this statement offers profound truth and should cause each of us to think a bit deeper about how we respond to the challenges in our lives. Many times, our reactions make all the difference, holding the power to radically change the course of our existence. I cannot always control what happens to me, but I can always control my own response.

It's okay to have different opinions.

With that, I also gained perspective about what it means to gracefully disagree. While differences of opinion exist within politics, religion, economics, medicine, education, and almost every other arena, I pray for the day when we can collectively arrive at a place of mutual respect. People are generally good, but sometimes it takes asking God for a particular gift to discern the divine qualities in another. I like how C. S. Lewis described it. He said, "There are no *ordinary* people. You have never talked to a mere mortal. Nations, cultures, arts, civilizations—these are mortal, and their life is to ours as the life of a gnat. But it is immortals whom we joke with, work with, marry, snub, and exploit."[15] I see truth in this statement. I subscribe to the notion that each of us is a child of God and that those temporary elements that divide mankind will one day be erased. It is then that we will at last see one another the way He sees us. Then, and perhaps only then, will we be able to interact with others with "no flippancy, no superiority, no presumption."[16]

Sometimes in life, we must be intentional and fervent about crowding out our own doubts.

For me, the first step in this process is to recognize when feelings of anger or bitterness begin to take root. Once, twice, or a thousand times a day, we each must decide that we don't want to go through life living under a cloud of negativity. When Peter the disciple walked on water, his gaze was at first fixed upon the Savior. It was only when he noticed the waves and roaring wind that fear began to occupy the place in his mind where faith had just resided, and he began to sink, saying, "Lord, save me!" (Matthew 14:30, KJV).

Who among us has not had occasion to cry out to God for help when we are sinking into despair? We cry to God because He has the ability to change us. He has felt our sorrows. As the Bible tells us, the Lord is "a man of sorrows, and acquainted with grief" (Isaiah 53:3, KJV). Thus, being acquainted with grief, He is acutely aware of the people and the experiences that can heal us, and His omnipresent yet anonymous hands work to bring them about when we ask.

Faith and patience are integral to the human experience.

My religious commitment and my devotion to living out my faith on the mission field became crucial components to get me through my severe injuries. Yet I feel that faith is something that must be nurtured carefully or it may wither as a small neglected flower in the heat of the sun. Though I persevered and never lost sight of the Lord, the daily grind of the physical recovery and the emotional fallout certainly took a toll. I have heard others describe life as a test to see if we will be able to bend our will to eventually merge with God's. While I still have a long way to go to become the type of person I one day wish to be, the recovery process has taught me the power of perseverance while simultaneously helping me to learn to depend on my faith.

Despite the pain and turmoil that resulted from those attacks, I persevered, didn't lose my faith, and refused to harbor anger—but it was only my anchored faith that made all of that possible. And I certainly wasn't perfect at those things all the time. Overcoming it all hasn't been easy; it's all collectively been a test of endurance that has shown me the power and value of the human spirit.

None of us are immune to sometimes facing internal questions and challenges surrounding our faith. And in my own experience, I truly have leaned on unity and peace to push through, which only forgiveness can usher in. Recognizing that we are angry or bitter and facing those feelings head-on is the first step to finding peace in times of difficulty. And making a concerted decision that we don't want to feel that way is the sure conduit to eventually putting off those negative feelings.

In the end, and as my friend and fellow survivor Richard Norby put it, I decided to be a survivor, not a victim. I made a conscious decision to have hope that things would work out, even when I had profound doubts about the details and about what my future would hold. That hope brought about faith to work through the doubts that I did have. Such faith can bring about the healing remedy of the Savior's love—a love that surpasses all understanding. Jesus has the ability to change us in the most profound ways, because He has literally felt every single thing we have ever felt. He knows the people and the experiences that can heal us, and His hands work about to make them happen when we ask.

Rather than speaking out of fear or anger, we all must seek a more tranquil and God-filled world; Jesus is the centerpiece of that paradigm.

Frustration is a part of life.

I've had some big frustrations and disappointments, which include coping with the injuries I sustained on my hand

and ankle—injuries that have been healing quite slowly. In my weaker moments, the long recovery and lingering issues made me wonder what was wrong with my body to make it heal so slowly. With my hand, I constantly had to change my glove and apply treatments; it's been an incessant reminder of what happened in the airport that day, one that I've been unable to escape. I would be lying if I said that overcoming the physical, spiritual, and emotional scars wasn't an everyday struggle to bring myself back to where I was before the attack. Feeling fragile and weak is something that was previously unfamiliar to me—and navigating it has been a trying experience.

If I'm being entirely honest, I have found myself incredibly frustrated. At the inability to do things, the time it was taking to feel better, at the sometimes bleak outlook life seemed to have. Life during my recovery was very difficult, as I struggled to get back into the swing of things. And, in the end, I'm certainly not the same person I was before. Many of us face a variety of circumstances that profoundly change us—and that's what happened to me in Brussels. Due to my injuries, there were some things that I simply couldn't do as well as I could before, and that was difficult to process and accept. Emotionally, there was also a noticeable impact, as I didn't necessarily communicate the same way I did before for a time. It was hard for me to connect with people emotionally for a while. I could be distrustful of people and their intentions as a result of suffering at the hands of strangers. But I decided early on that I wouldn't let the negatives of that day, or any day, define me.

To be frank, it was difficult. And I asked the Lord for help constantly. I realized that I just had to come to grips with those changes and accept that they were there as I tried to figure out how I could fix them, overcome them, or learn to be content with them. The emotional wounds were no less valid and serious than my physical wounds. If I didn't beat myself up for having a ruptured Achilles tendon, why would I beat myself up for being wary of people? Both were symptoms of the attack, and both were treatable. I was lucky to have the heavenly and earthly support systems that I did. They helped me stay rooted in myself, and they were patient as I navigated the tricky waters of emotional recovery.

Faith is everything.

One of the other challenges that emerged from my survival surrounded a question: Why me? It wasn't so much about me wondering why the events had to impact me and not someone else, rather the curiosity, which at moments plagued me, centered on a deep and profound uncertainty. I simply didn't know why I was alive while others who were standing right next to me were killed.

I still don't have all the answers to that question, though I do believe that there were certainly miracles that sustained and protected me that day. When I think back on the people who were around me when the first bomb detonated in the airport, I remember ordinary travelers and patrons just like myself. I know that among them were tourists whom I had helped at that Delta kiosk. I remember seeing a few businessmen. I remember seeing a family or two with kids. I remember the little play pad with a wooden plane right next to where I was in line. There were toddlers gleefully playing on it. When the explosion shattered those innocent scenes, I felt so utterly alone.

Why them and not me remains a profound mystery. But as Paul once said, "Now faith is the substance of things hoped for, the evidence of things not seen" (Hebrews 11:1, KJV). Faith is hope. And sometimes, hope is the only thing we can cling to, as it holds the power to persist amid every failure and uncertainty and regardless of any circumstance. We can't always answer the "why" in our lives, but God can give us the strength, courage, and peace to cope with whatever happens as we trust that He will use whatever has unfolded for His greater plan.

Faith, not doubt, yields the peace that we crave in times of tragedy and the assurance that everything will be all right. To me, that's why *faith is everything*. It dictates the way we look at our past, our future aspirations, our dreams, and our current needs. Faith comes by choice. Having hope is a decision; living it out is the most profound life goal. As a sometimes pessimistic person before these experiences, I now fully know that choosing to have hope is the surest way to be happy. And while I'm by no means a naturally courageous person, the strength and courage I do have is based on knowing that God's plan extends beyond the physical realm and the barriers that we have on this side of heaven.

It is my prayer that you will come away from this book with a renewed determination to consider the way you think about others, especially those who have wronged you. I'm far from perfect, but choosing to forgive has made me a happier person, helping me to move on and reclaim my life after facing the most unimaginable of circumstances.

131

The decision to want to put off anger and bitterness begins a process of healing that only a loving Father in Heaven can bring about. It doesn't begin by just instantaneously putting it off. It starts, however, with a simple desire to get to a better emotional place. Without that desire, forgiveness is impossible, unachievable, and inconceivable. Without embarking on a sincere quest to forgive, chasing that goal will always be just that: a chase. Something miraculous happens when we bring God into the equation. He answers the desires of a sincere heart.

I had a choice after surviving in the airport that day: I could have become bitter and angry because of my circumstances, questioning why God would have allowed them— or I could have wholeheartedly accepted what I was going through and relied on the Lord for strength. When I opted for the latter, I chose to be hopeful, rather than cynical. Being cynical would have been so, so easy, but it would have set me on an infinitely longer road to peace. I didn't want to mistrust the One who had given me so much. As a result, I found myself able to focus on the future, on recovery, and on the kind of person I wanted to become.

A life of sullenness was not one I wanted to lead. It may be that my desire to forgive was a special kind of mercy sent to keep me from harboring the rage that may eventually destroy me. I knew that I could not change the past or prevent destruction, but I could choose emancipation from any poisonous "root of bitterness" (Hebrews 12:15, KJV) and free myself from those feelings that would only keep me down.

I wonder if too many of us choose to live in the past rather than face the future with faith. Perhaps we let our yesterdays hold us hostage to such an extent that we are not able to press forward. I was laid low, lower than I've ever been, by my injuries. I couldn't do the things I loved to do or even do the things I needed to do, like walk and stand. But that has only made me appreciate the important things. I cannot say how grateful I am that I can *walk*. That I can run and stand and jump and climb and do anything I want. I find myself paying more attention to the things that really matter—that I am alive today, that I can be with my family, that I have made a full recovery, and that I know that the Savior lives. Even in moments of frustration, I am incredibly blessed. Remembering my blessings has this incredible way of making frustration fade away. The Lord preserved me when I was ten feet away from a bomb. He has been with me every step of the way, and He is not about to abandon me now.

I am changed, that is for certain. But the fundamentals of who I am were not changed. The person we've been throughout our entire lives, the things we've experienced, the relationships we've made—they're not lost or abandoned simply because a new chapter opens. We certainly can, and in many cases should, work toward personal change, but the lessons from that former self are certainly worth remembering. For example, moving to a different part of the country, starting at a new school, starting at a new job, raising a new family, starting life as a newlywed—these changes build upon who we currently are and refine our character. We have to have a sure foundation.

This concept also reminds me that the good I've done isn't lost tomorrow simply because I've made a mistake or done something bad—and just because I'm weak now doesn't mean I'm a weak person; I've done strong things in the past. Just because I have made a mistake does not mean that I am diminished or that my worth is less; I can always change for the better. I think our ability to look back on the road already traveled and to acknowledge the bad *and* the good is what will ultimately bring us happiness.

When we can look back on what we've said, done, and contributed and realize that we might have made some mistakes along the way—that the road might not have been paved out perfectly flat in some areas—we can gain some deeply profound perspective. And what we always have in front of us, no matter what mistakes we've made in the past, is a new road to pave. It's a new start, and a new beginning.

We are the difference that the world needs to become a better place. We can change others' lives and our own through small actions and, more pointedly, through forgiveness. It didn't take seeing heroes for me to learn that simple and heroic acts can change the trajectory of things.

My own story in Brussels is filled with examples of simple acts of selflessness that sustained and encouraged me throughout the ordeal. We don't have to move mountains to make a change; sometimes it takes a simple act of kindness and love to make all the difference.

CHAPTER 11 |
Lessons in Love |

Love is patient, love is kind. It does not envy, it does not boast, it is not proud. It does not dishonor others, it is not self-seeking, it is not easily angered, it keeps no record of wrongs. Love does not delight in evil but rejoices with the truth. It always protects, always trusts, always hopes, always perseveres.

(1 Corinthians 13:4–8, NIV)

There are countless books, films, songs, and plays about love. Those regarded as some of the greatest thinkers, philosophers, and artists in the world have written and spoken of its virtues. Gandhi proclaimed, "There only is life where there is love."[17] The Beatles sang, "All you need is love."[18]

J. K. Rowling's successful Harry Potter series is based on the eternal sacrifice of a mother's love. Perhaps some of the most revered biblical verses are the Apostle Paul's description of love: "And now these three remain: faith, hope and love. But the greatest of these is love" (1 Corinthians 13:13, NIV).

For Christians, the crowning example—indeed the very definition of love—was the Lord Jesus Christ's sacrifice on behalf of all humankind. "Greater love hath no man than this," he declared, "that a man lay down his life for his friends." He then added, "Ye are my friends" (John 15:13–14, KJV). In another example, the Bible implies that the Lord is the embodiment of loving attributes to such an extent that, "God *is* love" (1 John 4:8; emphasis added).

For centuries, believers and scholars alike have wrestled with the reconciliation of God's love and human suffering. "If God is love," some may ask, "then why do the innocent suffer? Why are war, terror, and destruction as consistent as the sunrise? What about the millions of suffering children, hungry and orphaned? Or the physical, mental, and emotional anguish endured by many?" Man's inhumanity to man litters the history of every nation. Suffering is not new, terror is not new, and life has always been and always will be fragile. There may be no satisfactory answer (at least from the present human perspective) to the dilemma of a world where love and hate coexist.

From the horrors of the Holocaust to thousands of years of religious conflict to personal and institutional racism, humankind's history of hate is as incomprehensible as it is real. Yet to deny hate and evil's existence would be to deny the existence of love. Given my brushes with terror, hate, and evil, I suppose I could choose to conclude that God does not exist. Or perhaps that He does not love His children anymore. I could choose to believe that perhaps God is no longer able to intervene on behalf of His children.

I have opted to use the word *choose* because I believe the *choice* to be an individual one; to exercise faith is an individual choice that must be made, renewed, and sustained. Still, I choose to believe that God does intervene because I have felt His interventions on my behalf.

While evil, despair, and suffering are guaranteed in this life, so too are faith, hope, and love. I have learned that if we let the weeds of doubt and despair overtake our minds, it is difficult for the flowers of faith to mature. Of necessity, the cultivation of faith takes constant weeding, "for as he thinketh in his heart, so is he" (Proverbs 23:7, KJV). As Martin Luther King Jr. said, "I have decided to stick with love. Hate is too great a burden to bear."[19] I believe that the burden of hate is compounded when we allow the evil actions of others to dictate our attitudes and approach to life. Why are some referred to as "terrorists"? Because they produce extreme fear and panic in the world. In my estimation, our sinking into despair is an acknowledgment of defeat. During the impending destruction of World War II, Winston Churchill spoke these famous words to rally his countrymen:

> We shall go on to the end. We shall fight in France, we shall fight on the seas and oceans, we shall fight with growing confidence and growing strength in the air, we shall defend our island, whatever the cost may be. We shall fight on the beaches, we shall fight on the landing grounds, we shall fight in the fields and in the streets, we shall fight in the hills; we shall never surrender.[20]

Our fight, the fight against evil and hate, rages on. Though military might is occasionally necessary and the policing of evil acts of hate will be constant, on an individual level, like Dr. King, I choose love, for my experiences with hate have only increased my desire to foster and solicit an enhancement of the virtue of love.

For me, the biblical attributes of faith, hope, and love are inseparable. I cannot speak of love without also including the other two virtues. The phrase, "God is love" denotes faith and hope in a divine being who is both omniscient and omnipresent. Therefore, to me, the power of love is not limited to the confines of reason or worldly wisdom. Nor is love relegated to the earth alone. In fact, sacred, spiritual experiences have led me to conclude that the love of God is beyond our comprehension and that the injustices of life will eventually be settled. How could man be held in judgment for hateful and evil acts if he was not free to choose? How could he choose God and love if he was coerced or could not comprehend the nature of what options he was choosing between?

Within each of my experiences with terror, saintly individuals, motivated by love, chose to look beyond themselves and serve others in need. These acts suggest to me that love is more than lip service. Love is more than longing for a better world. Love is demonstrated and enhanced through service.

The seeds of love were sown within me from a young age. I am the product of loving parents, siblings, and extended family members and a faith cultivated by years of exposure to Christian principles. I was taught the joys of service, sacrifice, and the fruits of hard work from my childhood. Lessons on love and service usually did not come by lecture, but from what could be called "the eloquence of example." I learned more from what I saw others do than what I heard others say.

One example that I recall vividly is at my grandfather's house in Ohio during the summer of 2014. Returning from an event, my grandfather parked the car and we started walking toward the front door. I remember feeling the heat of the Ohio sun combined with suffocating humidity. I only had one thing on my mind: getting inside as quickly as possible. But not my grandfather. He noticed a landscaper working diligently on a neighbor's yard. The man looked tired and worn from working in the heat of a midwestern summer. Grandpa went inside the house, filled up a large container of water, and offered it to the man. They talked in the shade for a few minutes before the landscaper continued his work. I'll always remember that day—it was a simple act of service that I wouldn't have thought to do. In fact, I hadn't even noticed the man.

I occasionally think back on this experience and wonder how often I have passed a fellow traveler in life's journey without lending a helping hand. How often have I been absorbed in my own desires and problems? How many times have I heard a sermon without taking it to heart and extending a hand of fellowship and love to someone else? I think this is what James meant in the New Testament when he defined what pure religion is. He said, "Pure religion and undefiled before God and the Father is this, to visit the fatherless and widows in their affliction, and to keep himself unspotted from the world" (James 1:27, KJV). I believe that James is trying to help us understand that all of the preaching in the world will amount to nothing unless we are willing to put forth real effort and actually live our religion. Jesus said,

Seeing Sister Clain for the first time after the attack.

"Inasmuch as ye have done it unto one of the least of these my brethren, ye have done it unto me" (Matthew 25:40, KJV). And again, "By this shall all men know that ye are my disciples, if ye have love one to another" (John 13:35, KJV). I was taught to "do a good turn daily" through my involvement with Boy Scouts. I am here today because of good turns done on my behalf. Although nothing could have adequately prepared me for a personal confrontation with evil and hate, witnessing the heroic sacrifice of others amidst terror and danger strengthened the faith of my youth. From observing the paramedics of Boston, the hospice of Paris, and the angelic figure of the stranger at Brussels, I experienced a hope in humankind more powerful than the selfish acts of some. In those times, love made more of an impact on me than the hatred ever did. These experiences have strengthened my resolve to spread love in the world.

A missionary experience may be referred to as a labor of love. Regardless of religious affiliation (or a lack thereof), a missionary's task is to spread goodwill and service throughout the world. Above all, missionaries are taught to love the people they serve and that the love they feel will increase proportionately to the amount of service they render. When

I left my family, friends, employment, and education to dedicate two years of my life to daily service (which began at 6:30 a.m. and ended at 10:30 p.m.), I knew that I had to work hard and learn to love people who are different from me. While I knew in my head that I needed to serve people, it was when I had a heartfelt desire to serve them that I saw the most difference. I could feel the love of God flow through me. I learned that "if any man will *do* his will, he shall *know* of the doctrine" (John 7:17, KJV; emphasis added). The accumulation of positive experiences before the Brussels attacks, both before and during my mission, were instrumental in rekindling my faith in mankind. Although I had had two previous encounters with hate, my many experiences with loving people were enough to drench any doubt in the general goodness of humankind.

Ironically, it may be more difficult to fully demonstrate love during times of peace and when one is not serving a full-time mission. Extreme events or time specifically set apart for Christian service are temporary reminders to look outward instead of inward. Quiet daily familial love, avoiding gossiping on social media, and personal daily worship are less noticeable than extreme acts of heroism. Especially when performed with anonymity, small acts of service may even go unreciprocated and unappreciated. Nevertheless, Christ gave two great commandments: "Thou shalt love the Lord thy God with all thy heart, and with all thy soul, and with all thy mind. This is the first and great commandment. And the second is like unto it, Thou shalt love thy neighbor as thyself" (Matthew 22:37–40, KJV).

Jesus's words suggest that above all else one does or fails to do, the love of God and neighbor are the greatest attributes one can develop. Would individuals commit any wrong—much less murderous atrocities—if the love of God and mankind was always in one's heart? Is there an evil act that could not be thwarted by the adherence to this brief declaration? Would any of the other commandments or directives from the Lord be necessary if humankind honored these words? I submit that the power of love, in conjunction with faith and hope, is the only power under heaven that can ultimately save mankind. Though I was motivated to openly declare the love and goodness of God for two years of Christian service in a foreign land to a people I did not know, I was the one who was the subject of divine tutoring. Now, every day, although I am very imperfect, I strive to be a little better, a little kinder, and a little more loving.

I try to measure my progress of self-development, not as a way to earn God's love or the praise of man, but with the measuring stick of love as Paul described it:

> Love is patient, love is kind. It does not envy, it does not boast, it is not proud. It does not dishonor others, it is not self-seeking, it is not easily angered, it keeps no record of wrongs. Love does not delight in evil but rejoices with the truth. It always protects, always trusts, always hopes, always perseveres. Love never fails. (1 Corinthians 13:4–8, NIV)

Though these verses are not new, they have taken on new meaning for me since my experiences with both hate and love amid the three terror attacks.

Love is patient, love is kind.

Since my brushes with terror I have learned to slow down a little. I believe some of the most sincere acts of service are to be patient and fully present with someone, to really listen and respond in kindness. Our hectic lifestyles and the compelling desire to accumulate more, and faster, often lead to a selfish hurriedness that is the antithesis of patience. There has been a reawakening inside me for what is most important in life, and a simple act of kindness and patience with another's perceived shortcomings is perhaps the pinnacle of living a life of service.

It does not envy, it does not boast, it is not proud.

I know my experiences with hate have the potential to drive away true love. I could envy others who have never had to deal with the trauma of terror or a painful recovery (both physically and psychologically). Or, I could be boastful and proud, suggesting that I am somehow better than someone who hasn't experienced what I've gone through. These feelings would drive away love and thus Paul's admonition to avoid them. Instead, I do my best to focus on my blessings. I have been the recipient of countless examples of love. It is through the assistance of a thousand loving hands that I have been able to cultivate a positive outlook and broader perspective. What have I, or any of us, to boast about when our very lives, and each day, are a gift from above?

It does not dishonor others, it is not self-seeking, it is not easily angered, it keeps no record of wrongs.

I take less offense at the actions of other people since the attack. The old saying "no one is perfect" is something we apply to other people, but seldom to ourselves. I've learned that many arguments are useless and do nothing more than put more enmity in between us and our peers. I've also learned that criticism rarely advances anything in life. There's no reason to gossip or degrade the character of other people. These things damage others and damage our character. On the flip side, I've learned that investing in other people despite their weaknesses brings lasting relationships that can lead to true meaning in life. People look over our weaknesses, and we should afford them the same. Now to be completely clear, I'm not talking about the difference between good and bad. The humanity inside each of us appeals to good, and we know when we're doing something we shouldn't. Drugs and other substances may hamper our ability to discern between good and bad choices, but as human beings we understand what it means to do good to our fellow men.

What terrorists did in Boston and Brussels was evil—it was wretched, it was wrong, and I believe they deserve to be punished as God sees fit. As for justice, though, I leave that to Him. As someone who firmly believes that God will make up for every wrong, I do my best to make the best decisions and trust that things will work out. I don't dwell on achieving "justice," because, for me, it doesn't change anything. I just move forward and remember that tomorrow is the first day of the rest of my life, and I can begin changing that life immediately.

Love does not delight in evil but rejoices with the truth.

The truth is that humankind is generally good. Each of us is endowed with divine attributes that must be nourished and refined, but each of us is endowed nonetheless. Though I acknowledge evil for what it is, I do not delight in it or dwell on it. It is a daily choice to rise above the evil, accentuate the good, and sincerely rejoice with truth wherever it is found. I believe that while many of us do not necessarily choose to delight in evil, its weight becomes an obstacle to our faith, hope, and love.

A preoccupation with evil and the problems of the world may lead to despondency, whereas the development of a positive outlook is contagious to others. I have had the opportunity to testify of God's redeeming love to others since the tragedies. These experiences have simply given me an enlarged sphere of influence where I can rejoice with others and strengthen the faith of others regarding His ultimate plan and our purpose on earth.

It always protects, always trusts, always hopes, always perseveres.

I am not sure how individuals can endure traumatic life experiences without faith in a higher power and a higher plan. For me, the ability to continue to persevere is directly associated with my ability to trust and hope, always. When filled with trust and hope, my desire to protect the innocent, as well as righteous principles, in a spirit of love is enhanced.

Love never fails.

Though we may fail at times, love will not. Just as I have learned that "a soft answer turneth away wrath" (Proverbs 15:1, KJV), so too does love extinguish hate. In the ultimate sense, when the final verdict has been read, I believe there will be no injustice. God is merciful and kind, but He is also just. He will never fail us as we trust in Him. It is my faith that when all accounts are settled, those who spread their own gospels of hate, bring terror to the innocent, and viciously seek to destroy that which is good and right will reap the rewards of their works. There is evil in the world, conniving and malicious, yet God will ever be there. Though my trials have been wrenching, they have awakened me to a greater sense that God's love is sure and steadfast.

Perhaps some readers will question why I must speak of God and love as inextricably linked. It is because I believe that all good and all love emanate from Him. He is love. After all, "Greater love hath no man than this, that a man lay down his life for his friends" (John 15:13, KJV).

CHAPTER 12
My Response to Terror

Let no man pull you so low as to hate him.

—Martin Luther King Jr.[21]

One of the most challenging elements in a situation like mine is that I won't ever have the chance to confront my attackers. Sure, I have chosen forgiveness, and I've committed to let love triumph over all else, but that doesn't alleviate the questions that still pop up in my head from time to time.

Without a doubt, the terrorists who mercilessly attacked the Brussels airport were consumed by their unrestrained hatred—so much so that they willingly died in a desperate attempt to end, destroy, or, at the least, forever change the lives of so many. "Why?" doesn't begin to capture my ongoing confusion and pain over that choice, that act of free will that forever changed my course.

I've often thought about what I would say to these men if given an opportunity, and since I'll never have that chance to look them in the eye and ask so many of the burning questions I'd love answered, I penned a letter directly to them—a cathartic experience that allowed me to fully express the multitude of emotions I feel when I think about their horrific cowardice.

Here it is:

> You must know that what you did was morally abhorrent, and it's evident from your actions that you were deceived by evil, having given in to the twisted hatred that plagues the souls of men. You both ruined and ended lives—meaningful lives.
>
> In the end, your actions made it ever-clear that you don't deserve to share this earth with good men and women. If I'm being honest, I'm glad both of you have moved toward God's judgment. You most certainly deserve the wrath of the Lord, but you also deserve His mercy. I hope that the morbid and vile tendencies you carry, to whatever extent they may be, are somehow changed, as you realize the gravity of who you have become.
>
> But make no mistake: Despite my harsh feelings about your acts, I have forgiven both of you. That, of course, doesn't make what you did permissible. It never will be. I—along with every freedom-loving and rational person across this globe—condemn what you did in the strongest terms, but I have chosen not to allow hate to overtake my heart for either of you.
>
> I know that there is value in life, and I hope that you can go on living in the next life as happy as possible given what you've done and

the heavy regret that will most certainly sit on your hearts. I hope one day that we can meet, so you can know that good has indeed come in the wake of your evil acts.

Cordially,

Mason Scott Wells, a Survivor

This letter carries with it the spirit and overall scope of this book. In the end, I want you to walk away from *Left Standing* with a firmer grip on faith, hope, and forgiveness. I want you to see through my own journey that it is absolutely possible to replace the anger and hate in our hearts and lives with unwavering love—and that even when we struggle with certain parts of life, there is always a valuable lesson for us to learn, even if its buried deep in the weeds. Good can most certainly come out of the worst of experiences.

The blast taught me that God loves all of His children unconditionally—something I believe as much as I know that the sun will rise tomorrow. I've learned that God's love extends far enough to allow us to experience hard and even tragic events in our lives, while coming out on the other side refined.

I have also learned that God's choice to give us complete freedom over our will is actually an expression of His love for us; like a good parent, He allows us to pave our own destiny, though He is willing to step in and guide the trajectory so long as we invite Him into our lives to do so. He stepped in with my life, and I'm forever grateful that He did.

Surviving terror and enduring the lengthy recovery has fortified my belief that, while God may want certain things for our lives and may even prepare a pathway to accomplish such things, ultimately, we define who we are and what we become by the choices and decisions we make. Will we pave our paths under the guidance of His perfect love? Or will we follow the path of darkness and solitude? That's the choice we must make.

The events in Boston and Brussels made my family stronger. While my parents were pushed to their limits both mentally and emotionally, they learned to rely on God and trust in good people in order to do what they otherwise couldn't have accomplished on their own. They, like me, have learned that it's okay to accept that we have limits. I had to recognize many times during my recovery that there were things I simply couldn't do on my own. I did my best to push the limits, but at the same time, I recognized when I had done all that I could do.

There are many ideological differences in today's world. As good citizens, the responsibility is ours to respect those differences insomuch as they do not infringe upon our constitutional and God-given rights. In the face of so much turmoil in the world today, it's easy to be shortsighted and intolerant of what others believe. I know from experience. As a missionary, my faith was attacked and criticized constantly. The insults people hurled at me were misguided and usually very uninformed, but that didn't stop them.

In the end, the slurs and insults never bothered me. Instead, they taught me a valuable lesson, illustrating that there are times in which human beings might not understand another person or group. Sometimes, rather than approaching differences or foreign concepts with respect and inquisitiveness, we are prone to dismissing and going after what others believe. As a result of my experiences, I find myself slower to criticize than I did before. Critique is necessary in life, but when it extends into harassment and diminishment of others, the infractions not only harm others, but also degrade our own character.

These are themes that we can all relate to. Adversity is unique to no one. And no one is immune to it either. There will be times in each of our lives when we need to overcome something that we fear is bigger than ourselves. In the face of challenges, tragedy, and trials, we must remind ourselves that we *can* overcome the barriers in our lives. Embracing adversity when it comes our way, rather than seeking to avoid it, will remind us that we can and we will succeed. The line that separates success from failure in every scenario is attitude, not outcome.

As I embark on the next chapter in my life, I'm looking forward to the future that I at one point feared wouldn't be possible. In ten years, I envision myself serving as an officer in the US military, continuing to defend this great nation and its citizens. I've learned so much, yet I know that there's still much to work on. In time, I hope that I will be a better role model and a more empathetic person. I hope that peace will be more uniform throughout the globe and I hope that I can contribute to that movement. I hope that I will be a better listener and a better friend. I hope to have a family and raise my children in a way that will guide them to be good, prosperous, and determined people. I hope to better accept my weaknesses, and I hope to build upon them. I hope that I will always be a missionary, sharing the good news of the Lord.

Hope, of course, is the key.

AFTERWORD
by Tyler Beddoes

I met Mason when we both participated in America's Freedom Festival in Provo, Utah, in June of 2016. I followed Mason's story closely through the media when he was critically injured in the Brussels bombing. I remember feeling the proximity to home was really concerning. Although the bombing was in distant Belgium, Mason's home was not far from mine. I remember feeling the heartache and praying for him and everyone affected. Mason offered the prayer at the Freedom Festival event that evening, and I was filled with gratitude that only three months after this attack, he was standing there in fairly good health offering a prayer. I felt the Spirit strongly and was moved by his words and positive attitude.

Meeting Mason was something that I will never forget. He had well-refined Christian virtues of kindness, patience, and endurance beyond his years. I remember shaking his left hand, since his right hand was in a glove and severely injured. You could see and feel his strength then and now. Mason's influence has made me a better person. To watch someone so young overcome so much tragedy in his life yet remain so positive was something I personally needed. His influence has helped me prioritize the most important things in life. Our lives can change in an instant, and for Mason, he chose to react to it in a positive way. With me being more pessimistic in nature, I most likely wouldn't have reacted in the way Mason did. Seeing what he had gone through and overcome while still maintaining a forgiving heart has strengthened my faith. Mason has shown me that we must forgive and continue on the path of life and keep our faith.

I am thankful that I got the opportunity to work with Mason on this book. Mason asked if I would help him put his story in words. I am forever grateful for the opportunity, and he may not truly know how much his strength has helped me. I am a full-time police officer, and the tunnel vision of negativity sometimes sets in. However, Mason's story has helped me remain positive through the difficult times. I coauthored a book called *Proof of Angels* which details the lowest and highest points of my faith. Working with Mason was just another stepping stone in my life that has helped increase my faith in God. We must try as children of God to rid ourselves of hate and negativity and generously offer the "garment of praise" (Isaiah 61:3). The abundant life, the joyful life, is to incrementally develop the attributes of the Divine. This task can appear daunting, yet Mason's message is the embodiment of hope—a hope in God and humanity.

It is my desire that everyone that reads this book also finds some solace in it and takes a piece out of Mason's journey and applies it into their own lives. I hope readers truly find hope. Each day offers a new opportunity to be a loving husband to my beautiful wife and a father to three precious children and teach them that we must have hope and keep our faith in God in all things, even when times are extremely difficult. One of the greatest bands of all time, Journey, sums this up with the line "Don't stop believin', hold on to that feelin'."[22] If we keep God on our minds and in our hearts at all times, we can get through anything!

—Tyler Beddoes

APPENDIX |
The Facts |

What follows is a brief description of each of the terror attacks discussed in this book:

Boston

The Tsarnaev brothers detonated two bombs at the finish line of the Boston Marathon. The attack killed three people and injured 260 others. Sixteen of those injured souls lost limbs. Days later, while attempting to flee from law enforcement, the Tsarnaev brothers led police on a manhunt that included a murdered police officer, a hostage situation, and the eventual death of one of the suspects in a violent shootout with police. Although the younger brother temporarily escaped, he was soon arrested after being discovered hiding in a resident's boat.

The detonation of the bombs disrupted an otherwise peaceful afternoon when runners and spectators gathered from many nations to participate and witness the historic Boston Marathon. The Boston Marathon originated on April 19, 1897, as an all-male, 24.5-mile race involving eighteen runners, partly as a salute to Patriot's Day, which memorialized the beginning of the Revolutionary War.[23] Since its inception, the marathon has become one of the most prestigious races in the world, with thirty thousand athletes gathering each year to participate.[24]

However, the 117th iteration of the race in 2013 stands apart—living on in both infamy and honor as two deranged killers sought to destroy life while thousands more gathered to celebrate it.

The murderers carefully planned the attacks with pre-meditated intent to rob innocent life as a proclaimed public response to American military action across the world. The bombs were created using pressure cookers filled with shrapnel and disguised in backpacks. The backpacks were strategically placed in a crowded space to inflict maximal damage to onlookers of the race. Among the three victims was an eight-year-old boy and a nine-year-old girl sustaining injuries that required a leg amputation.[25]

Though the detonation of the two bombs caused relatively little structural damage, the physical and mental scars still remain for all who witnessed the events personally or by media. Since September 11, 2001, when nearly three thousand people lost their lives and countless others sustained unspeakable physical and mental trauma, any terror attack on American soil represents a wound to the entire nation as well as nations of goodwill across the world. Though on a much smaller scale than 9/11, the Boston attacks with the destruction from two pressure-cooker bombs served as a reminder that terror can strike on American soil and that evil and cunning individuals continue to spread their gospel of hate.

Paris

On Friday, November 13, 2015, the horrors of terrorism visited the ancient city of Paris. On this fateful day, between 9:20 p.m. and 9:53 p.m., 130 people lost their lives and 368 people were injured in a string of orchestrated events that included suicide bombings and mass shootings. Though the city was on frequent high alert for terrorism, nothing of its kind had transpired since WWII had ravished Europe. The attacks on Paris were not isolated to a single location but were organized in succession throughout the city. The first series of attacks occurred at the Stade de France sports stadium where France was hosting Germany in a soccer match. Three bombers, in roughly twenty-minute increments, detonated the bombs outside the stadium, killing themselves and others. Just minutes after the second bomb had detonated outside the stadium, attackers opened fire outside a restaurant, killing at least fifteen people and wounding several more. The shooting at the restaurant was carried out in conjunction with shootings at two additional restaurants. Prior to the third detonation at the stadium, a suicide bomber injured several more people at a downtown café. Additionally, three men opened fire for twenty minutes at a crowded concert and then held the remaining attendees hostage. The conflict ended when two of the men committed suicide and one was killed by police. The attacks in Paris heightened the anxiety of an already fear-ridden city and unleashed a series of air strikes targeting ISIS strongholds by French fighter jets following the declaration of a state of emergency by President Hollande.

The Paris attacks differed from the Boston bombings in two fundamental ways. First, the Paris attacks were orchestrated with one attack coinciding with another across the city, while the Boston bombings were primarily centralized. Second, the terrorists in Paris claimed allegiance to the Islamic State in Iraq and Syria (ISIS) while it was concluded that the Boston attacks were executed by two individuals acting independently.[26] The atrocities of Boston and Paris similarly represent attacks on the home front—the home front of two nations that for decades had largely assumed acts of terror as disturbing but distant. Now, no nation was entirely immune from the repeated acts of terror.

Brussels

On March 22, 2016, at 7:58 a.m., suicide bombers detonated two explosives just nine seconds apart in the Brussels Zaventem Airport. While citizens waited to check travel luggage, the explosions led to a sea of confusion and panic, shattering windows and destroying a departure terminal. The terrorists planted a third bomb but were unable to detonate it. Approximately an hour later, another explosion occurred in a metro station. These two attacks left thirty-two innocent people dead (seventeen at the airport and fourteen at the metro station) and more than three hundred injured.

Similar to the Paris attacks, the traumatic bombings were carried out through careful orchestration from a group of five murderers believed to operate in connection with ISIS.[27]

Like the Boston and Paris attacks, the terror at Brussels was an attack on all nations of goodwill; the targeting of an airport tactically produced casualties from multiple nations. The explosions in the departure terminal in the early spring of 2016 was the worst terror attack known to have occurred in Belgium.[28] The wounds caused by evil men still haunt this proud country.

ENDNOTES

1. Alexander Graham Bell, as quoted in Stephen Palmer, *The Pillars 4 Success* (Stone Mountain, GA: TPH Group, 2014), 63.

2. Martin Luther King Jr., *Strength to Love*, gift ed. (1977; repr., Minneapolis, MN: Fortress Press, 2010), 47.

3. Fred Rogers, *The Mister Rogers Parenting Book: Helping to Understand Your Young Child* (Philadelphia, PA: Running Press, 2002), 107.

4. Jeff Bauman and Bret Witter, *Stronger* (New York: Grand Central Publishing, 2014), 84.

5. Michael Jordan, as quoted in T. J. Allan, "How Michael Jordan's Mindset Made Him a Great Competitor," *USA Basketball*, November 24, 2015, www.usab.com/youth /news/2012/08/how-michael-jordans-mindset-made-him -great.aspx.

6. John Dewey, as quoted in Colin Beard and John P. Wilson, *Experiential Learning: A Handbook for Education, Training, and Coaching*, 3rd ed. (London: Kogan Page, 2013), 28.

7. Mark Banschick, "God, 'Why Have You Made Me Your Target'? (Job 7:20): How Religion Confuses—And How God Responds," *Psychology Today*, March 22, 2013, www.psychologytoday.com/blog/the-intelligent-divorce /201303/god-why-have-you-made-me-your-target -job-720.

8. Bear Grylls, as quoted in Dejan, "The Survivor Spirit," *Fearless Motivation*, April 21, 2016, www .fearlessmotivation.com/2016/04/21/bear-grylls-quotes.

9. Jeffrey R. Holland, "Face to Face with Jeffrey R. Holland," *Mormon Channel*, March 8, 2016, video, 1:53:49, www .mormonchannel.org/watch/series/face-to-face/face-to -face-with-elder-jeffrey-r-holland-1.

10. Lao Tzu, in *Tao Te Ching*, chapter 64.

11. Desmond TuTu, in Deborah Solomon, "The Priest," *New York Times*, March 4, 2010, www.nytimes.com/2010/03 /07/magazine/07fob-q4-t.html.

12. Zig Ziglar, *See You at the Top*, 25th anniversary ed. (Gretna, LA: Pelican Publishing Company, 2005), 199.

13. William Paul Young, *The Shack* (Newbury Park, CS: Windblown Media, 2007), 227.

14. See Thomas S. Monson, "Decisions Determine Destiny" (Brigham Young University devotional, November 6, 2005), speeches.byu.edu.

15. C. S. Lewis, *The Weight of Glory* (New York: HarperOne, 2001), 46.

16. Ibid.

17. Mahatma Gandhi, as quoted in "Essential Quotes of Mahatma Gandhi," Gandhi International Institute for

Peace, accessed August 24, 2017, gandhianpeace.com /quotes.html.

18. The Beatles, "All You Need Is Love," by Lennon–McCartney, recorded June 14, 1967, track 6 of *Yellow Submarine*, EMI and De Lane Lea studios.

19. Martin Luther King Jr., as quoted in Tony Castle, *A Treasury of Christian Wisdom* (London: Hodder and Houghton, 2001), 149.

20. Winston Churchill, "We Shall Fight on the Beaches" (speech), June 4, 1940, House of Commons, Parliament of the United Kingdom, transcript and audio, 12:13, www .winstonchurchill.org/resources/speeches/1940-the-finest -hour/we-shall-fight-on-the-beaches.

21. Martin Luther King Jr., as quoted in *A Knock at Midnight: Inspiration from the Great Sermons of Reverend Martin Luther King*, edited by Clayborne Carson and Peter Holloran (New York: Time Warner Books, 2000), 32.

22. Journey, "Don't Stop Believin'," by Steve Perry, Jonathan Cain, and Neal Schon, released June 3, 1981, Fantasy Studios.

23. "History of the Marathon," Boston Athletic Association, accessed August 25, 2017, www.baa.org/races/boston -marathon/boston-marathon-history.aspx.

24. "2017 Boston Marathon Statistics," Boston Athletic Association, accessed August 25, 2017, raceday.baa.org /statistics.html.

25. "Boston Marathon Bombings," History.com, accessed August 25, 2017, www.history.com/topics/boston -marathon-bombings.

26. "2015 Paris Terror Attacks Fast Facts," CNN.com, updated November 30, 2016, www.cnn.com/2015/12/08/europe/2015-paris-terror-attacks-fast-facts/index.html; "Paris Attacks: What Happened on the Night," *BBC News*, December 9, 2015, www.bbc.com/news/world-europe-34818994.

27. "Brussels Explosions: What We Know about Airport and Metro Attacks," *BBC News*, April 9, 2016, www.bbc.com/news/world-europe-35869985.

28. Charlotte McDonald-Gibson, "Fear and Frustration Continue One Year after Belgium's Worst Terror Attack," *TIME*, March 20, 2017, time.com/4707414/belgium-airport-terror-attack.

ABOUT THE AUTHORS

Mason Wells

Mason was born in Santa Maria, California, and moved to Utah when he was young. He graduated with honors from Lone Peak High School. Mason earned an Eagle Scout Award and traveled to Paris, France, where he served as a missionary. In the course of his service, he was severely injured in but survived the Brussels Airport bombing in March 2016. Since returning home, he has completed one year of college at the University of Utah and is now a midshipman at the United States Naval Academy, where he is studying engineering.

Tyler Beddoes

Tyler was born in Provo, Utah. He studied criminal justice and journalism at Utah Valley University. He joined the police department in Spanish Fork, Utah, in 2006. During his service with the Spanish Fork Police Department, he has received an Exemplary Service Award and was recognized by the mayor of Spanish Fork, the State of Utah, and the United States Congress for his involvement in the miraculous rescue of Lily Groesbeck from the Spanish Fork River on the morning of March 7, 2015. He is the coauthor of the book *Proof of Angels*. He currently resides in Utah with his wife, Brittany, and their three children.

Billy Hallowell

Through journalism, media, public speaking appearances, and the blogosphere, Billy Hallowell has worked as a journalist and commentator for nearly twenty years. He has been published and featured in countless political and cultural books, textbooks, articles, and websites. Hallowell was the faith and culture editor of *TheBlaze*, and he has contributed to the *Washington Post*, *Human Events*, *The Daily Caller*, *Mediaite*, *Deseret News*, and the *Huffington Post*, among other news sites. He is also the author of *The Armageddon Code* and *Fault Line*.